"*Including Learners with Medical Needs in School* is an excellent book that fills a crucial gap in education resources. Written in an easy-to-read style by a range of experts with significant knowledge and first-hand experience, it is packed with information, strategies, case studies, points for reflection and practical resources. I think this is an essential read for anyone committed to ensuring that children with medical needs flourish at school. Highly recommended!"

Natalie Packer, *SEND Consultant and Director, NPEC Ltd*

"The strength of *Including Learners with Medical Needs in School* lies not only in the expertise of its contributors but also in its accessible and easy to understand format. Each chapter provides practical strategies for supporting children with medical needs, covering everything from reintegration after illness, traumatic brain injuries to medication management and telepresence solutions. The book is designed to dip into as needed, making it a valuable, flexible resource for those busy in schools. Don't wait until you need this book, buy it to help create an inclusive school community by design."

Sarah Johnson, *President of PRUsAP, director of Phoenix Education Consultancy*

"This book is an excellent resource written by a range of professionals who have 'lived' experience of supporting children and young people with a range of medical and mental health needs. Throughout the book, alongside the legal responsibilities of who should do what, there are case studies which demonstrate how schools can put into practice outstanding support to ensure that their pupils feel 'wanted'. The area of education for pupils with medical needs is often misunderstood but this book provides clarity, and on reading and following the guidance all schools should feel better placed to support these children and young people. After all, most of them have one wish – not to be treated differently and to feel included alongside their peers."

Janice Cahill OBE, *Independent Consultant*

"This book is a must read for those working in education to understand the strategic and practical ways to support individuals with medical needs. This idea of it being a 'dip in ' book is exactly what busy SENDCOs need."

Ginny Bootman, *Specials Needs and Relationship Specialist, SENDCO, Keynote Speaker and Author of* Independent Thinking On Being A SENDCO

"I see so many schools that are rethinking their approach to children with medical needs. This is a timely resource that will give leaders confidence rooted in serious expertise to develop the culture of belonging in school. A well-researched book full of practical advice across all the essential areas – legal frameworks, medication support, injury recovery, psychological support, technology, curriculum approaches – to facilitate equitable planning and successful inclusion."

Margaret Mulholland, *SEND and Inclusion Specialist, Association of School and College Leaders*

Access your Online Resources

Including Learners with Medical Needs in School is accompanied by a number of printable online materials, designed to ensure this resource best supports your professional needs

Go to https://resourcecentre.routledge.com/speechmark and click on the cover of this book

Answer the question prompt using your copy of the book to gain access to the online content.

Including Learners with Medical Needs in School

This accessible book is packed with information and strategies that will build your confidence in ensuring that children and young people with medical needs have equal access to education and can thrive academically, socially, and emotionally.

Including Learners with Medical Needs in School provides school staff with a guide for best practice in supporting learners with complex health conditions in their schools. The book includes:

- An overview of legal considerations and the responsibilities of schools and local authorities
- How to create a welcoming environment and support the smooth reintegration to school following absences, as well as advice on managing medication and creating strong home–school partnerships
- Guidance on working effectively with hospital schools, medical alternative provision, paediatric hospitals, and mental health units
- A wealth of case studies, top tips, and tried-and-tested practical strategies that can be easily applied without huge costs or training
- Signposting to further resources as well as downloadable specimen polices, exemplar Individual Healthcare Plans, and training materials.

By implementing the recommendations in this book, schools can make a commitment to inclusion and make a real difference to the educational experience of children with medical needs. It is essential reading for SENCOs, pastoral leads, and senior leaders, as well as a useful resource for school governors and school nurses.

Cath Kitchen is an experienced leader in Alternative Provision for learners with medical needs, working alongside the Department of Education. She chairs the National Association for Hospital Education, provides school improvement advice, and was a pathfinder for the Ethical Leadership Framework. Cath has an OBE for services to children and young people.

Including Learners with Medical Needs in School

A Guide to Best Practice

Edited by Cath Kitchen

Routledge
Taylor & Francis Group

LONDON AND NEW YORK

Designed cover image: Charleigh Hollanby, Year 11

First published 2025
by Routledge
4 Park Square, Milton Park, Abingdon, Oxon OX14 4RN

and by Routledge
605 Third Avenue, New York, NY 10158

Routledge is an imprint of the Taylor & Francis Group, an informa business

British Library Cataloguing-in-Publication Data
A catalogue record for this book is available from the British Library

ISBN: 978-1-032-76538-9 (hbk)
ISBN: 978-1-032-76424-5 (pbk)
ISBN: 978-1-003-47894-2 (ebk)

DOI: 10.4324/9781003478942

Typeset in Optima
by Apex CoVantage, LLC

Access the Support Material: https://resourcecentre.routledge.com/speechmark

This book is dedicated to the amazing learners and their families who show great resilience every day in not only coping with their medical condition, but also in their determination to continue with their education, despite their challenges. It has truly been a privilege to have been able to work with you.

Contents

Acknowledgements   xv

List of contributors   xvi

1   **Introduction: The purpose of this book and
    how you might use it**   1
    Cath Kitchen

SECTION 1: THE LEGAL BIT   7

2   **The legal requirements**   9
    Cath Kitchen

3   **Individual Healthcare Plans**   17
    Cath Kitchen

4   **Local authority (LA) responsibilities**   24
    Cath Kitchen

**SECTION 2: BEST PRACTICE EXAMPLES OF HOW TO INCLUDE
LEARNERS WITH MEDICAL NEEDS IN YOUR SCHOOL**   29

5   **Checking for dragons and potholes: Creating
    a welcoming environment for learners with
    medical conditions**   31
    Tara Bell

6   **Promoting and supporting attendance**   41
     Simon Pini and Vicky Hopwood

7   **The psychological impact of attending school
     with a medical condition**   54
     Helen Griffiths

8   **The wider curriculum for learners with
     medical needs**   63
     James Gibson

9   **The use of telepresence solutions**   72
     Cath Kitchen and Penny White

10   **Working with your local hospital school/medical
     Alternative Provision**   81
     *Janet Doherty, Joanna Beswick. Emma Cunha,
     and Gwen Rees-Moffitt*

11   **Hidden in plain sight: Best practice for supporting
     learners with acquired brain injury (ABI)**   92
     Emily Bennett and Gemma Costello

12   **Managing medicines in educational settings**   110
     Nirusha Govender

13   **Best practice in supporting reintegration to
     school following a period of absence**   135
     James Shryane and Victoria Howard

SECTION 3: WORKING WITH HOSPITAL SETTINGS   147

14   **Supporting learners in paediatric hospitals**   149
     Jayne Franklin

15   **Supporting learners in Child and Adolescent
     Mental Health units**   161
     Karen Ingham and Lorraine Coady

SECTION 4: NEXT STEPS   **171**

16   **Children's health charities that can
provide advice, support, and resources**   **173**
*Cath Kitchen, Daniella Rotimi, Tracey Dunn, Rajwant Kaur
Singh, Sammie McFarland, Chelsea Wong, Tina Coope,
Catherine Hodder, Maria Marinho, and Michelle Allen*

17   **The Medical Needs in Schools project**   **184**
Steve Lowe

Index   *193*

Resources (available online)

Chapter 2

- Presentation for governors
- Whole school audit tool

Chapter 3

- Template for IHCP

Chapter 4

- Model LA policy

Chapter 6

- Self-reflection questions for school staff

Chapter 7

- More information on the top tips

Chapter 8

- Holistic progress tracker from Becton School

Chapter 10

– Links to websites with tools for gathering the voice of the learner

Chapter 11

– Leaflet on best practice for supporting learners with ABI

– Links to available training for schools on ABI

Chapter 12

– Case study: Award winning collaboration between special schools & NHS healthcare providers

– Links to resources referred to in Chapter 12

– Template A3 MAR chart

– Template for medicine errors reporting

– Template letter to community pharmacy to purchase AAIs

– Template letter to community pharmacy to purchase asthma inhalers

– Template medicines in school self-audit

– Template medicines information leaflet for parents

– Template parental consent form to administer medicines in school

– Template school trip medical consent letter

Chapter 13

– Links to resources referred to in Chapter 13

Chapter 16

– Additional resources information from children's health charities

Acknowledgements

Thank you to my supportive family for your wisdom, patience and unfailing faith in me, particularly my daughter Lynsey who set me on this path of a passion for providing education for learners with medical needs and whose resilience and determination are a constant source of inspiration to me.

Thank you to all the professionals who have so generously given of their time to contribute to this book, including those who are part of the National Association for Hospital Education, NHS colleagues and the children's health charities. Our shared vision and values have led to the content contained in the book and our passion to make a difference to learners with medical needs.

Contributors

Michelle Allen has worked at Versus Arthritis for the past two years as the Young People and Families Service Manager for England and has over 18 years' experience of working with children/young people and families. She thrives on their achievements and watching them flourish even when managing a long-term health condition.

Tara Bell is the LA advisor for learners with medical needs in Wandsworth and the headteacher of two outstanding hospital schools (mental health and general medical) and extended outreach services for learners out of school due to medical and/or mental health conditions, including EBSA (emotional based school avoidance).

Emily Bennett specialises in paediatric neuropsychology and neuroreha-bilitation and works clinically with learners and adolescents with acquired brain injury (ABI) and complex neurological, neuro-oncological and neu-rosurgical conditions. She also lectures on local Doctorate and Masters courses and works nationally to support the development of provision for learners with ABI in education. Emily is the current Chair for the National ABI in Learning and Education Syndicate (NABLES).

Joanna Beswick has over 20 years' experience working in primary main-stream and hospital education. As a senior leader, she has led on curriculum development and embedding high quality teaching and learning within hos-pital education. As an experienced coach, Joanna has supported teachers to develop their teaching practice using educational research. She is the current headteacher of Manchester Hospital School, leading educational provision for learners in hospitals, in the community and in homes across the area.

Lorraine Coady has over 20 years of teaching and leadership experience in Alternative Provision. With a broad background in mainstream and specialist provisions, Lorraine is passionate about multi-disciplinary collaboration and reflective practice. She is the national education lead for the Advisory Board CAMHS branch of the Royal College of Psychiatry. Lorraine is currently the headteacher at Simmons House CAMHS Unit, a specialised hospital school, where she is responsible for providing educational provision for all learners who are admitted to the hospital.

Tina Coope is a former teacher who has taught across both special and mainstream schools. Aged seven, Tina's daughter developed the sudden onset of severe neuropsychiatric symptoms. She rapidly required a TA and developed SEN. In 2020, Tina became the Education Lead for PANS PANDAS UK.

Gemma Costello specialises in paediatric neuropsychological rehabilitation and works with learners and their families, across home, school, and community, following acquired brain injury. She is also involved in national projects developing provision for learners with ABI in education and lectures on Doctoral and Masters courses on paediatric neuropsychology and acquired brain injury. Gemma is part of the National ABI in Learning and Education Syndicate (NABLES).

Emma Cunha has been working in education for 20 years, over half of this time in senior leadership as well as time as a SENDco and a trained senior mental health lead. The proud mother of children with both ADHD and Autism, she has experienced the school system from primary through to university from this point of view. Emma is currently the assistant headteacher at Manchester Hospital School.

Janet Doherty has worked as a teacher and in senior leadership roles in education for almost 40 years. Janet was the Executive Headteacher at Manchester Hospital School for 7 years. She utilises her valuable experience as a school leader, school improvement professional and Director of Education. She is now an Independent Education Consultant.

Tracey Dunn is the Education and AllergyWise® Manager, Anaphylaxis UK, and a retired headteacher and mum to children with allergies. Before joining the Anaphylaxis UK team, she supported them by being the Education Ambassador on a voluntary basis. She brings her wealth of education and allergy knowledge to support the allergic community to have a brighter future, advising education settings.

Jayne Franklin worked as a headteacher in both mainstream and specialist schools from 2004–2024 and is the previous head of Great Ormond Street and UCH Hospital School. She has experience at a national and local level in transforming school systems, implementing professional networks, designing policy, and driving strategic reviews enabling communities to grow and improve despite ever-growing social and economic challenges. Jayne is currently an Independent Education Consultant.

James Gibson has been a headteacher in hospital education for over 6 years and worked previously at a PRU for excluded learners. He currently sits on the DfE Headteacher Reference Group and is a director of the National Association of Hospital Education. James is the executive headteacher of the Becton School in Sheffield, part of the Nexus Trust, which provides education for learners at the hospitals and in the community

Nirusha Govender is a pharmacist with over 25 years' experience in community services. Nirusha is passionate about SEND and working towards equitable healthcare access. Over the last 15 years, Nirusha worked closely with NHS commissioners and senior leaders, local authorities and schools to develop an award-winning medicines management service in Kent. Nirusha is the Associate Director for Pharmacy Workforce, Medicines Quality & Safety, NHS Kent, and Medway Integrated Care Board, UK.

Helen Griffiths is a Consultant Clinical Psychologist and Head of Psychological Services, Great Ormond Street Hospital, and has a passion for raising the profile of the psychological needs of children with medical conditions and their families. She has chaired the UK Paediatric Psychology Network and worked with children and their families for over 15 years in a range of settings. Helen trained at the University of Oxford and continues to be very active across many aspects of professional development.

Catherine Hodder leads Young Epilepsy's work to improve systems of support for children and young people living with epilepsy. She is the Head of Voice, Policy and Influencing for Young Epilepsy, UK.

Vicky Hopwood delivers research and evaluation across education, health and social care. She specialises in qualitative research methods. The main focus of her work is the fields of special educational needs and disability, health and well-being, family support and inclusion, and digital health. Vicky is an experienced research fellow at the University of Leeds who has been supporting the study into the lived experiences of learners living with long-term physical health conditions.

Victoria Howard is a teacher with over 30 years' experience in education and has had the privilege of working and leading in primary, middle and secondary schools, across different local authorities. She is currently the headteacher at Cherry Tree Learning Centre, which is part of The Skylark Partnership Trust.

Karen Ingham is passionate about outcomes for vulnerable children and has been a senior leader since 2003 holding responsibilities including safeguarding, behaviour, teaching and learning. She has headship experience in mainstream and special school settings and is currently the headteacher of Cloughside College in Bury, a special hospital school based in a CAMHS unit, responsible for provision of education for all learners who are admitted to the hospital.

Cath Kitchen is an experienced leader in Alternative Provision for learners with medical needs, working alongside the Department of Education. She chairs the National Association for Hospital Education, provides school improvement advice, and was a pathfinder for the Ethical Leadership Framework. Cath has an OBE for services to children and young people.

Steve Lowe has held various senior leadership positions in mainstream secondary schools in London, Reading and Swindon also serving as an associate headteacher in an EOTAS/PRU. He works as a School Improvement Partner in Oxfordshire, is a Director at NAHE and is a member of the HCiSA. Steve is the headteacher of Oxfordshire Hospital School and is responsible for the provision of education at the different county hospital settings, and in the community.

Sammie McFarland is a passionate women's health expert and the CEO and founder of Long Covid Kids, the leading UK charity for children with Long Covid. Named a Coronation Champion in 2023, she has received multiple awards for her work. Sammie's lived experience, leadership and advocacy have significantly contributed to the paediatric Long Covid community.

Maria Marinho has worked in the field of hospital education for over 25 years. Latterly she has worked as part of a small team at Chelsea Community Hospital School designing, developing and promoting Well at School.

Simon Pini is an academic psychologist and in 2021 he commenced a National Institute for Health Research fellowship at the University of Leeds focusing on the school lives of learners living with long-term physical health conditions. Previously Simon worked as a Learning Mentor supporting education engagement for teenagers with cancer.

Gwen Rees-Moffitt is a SEND and literacy specialist and has worked in mainstream secondary schools for 18 years, leading on improving outcomes for disadvantaged learners. She recently made the move to hospital education and is now the strategic lead for SEND and Safeguarding at Manchester Hospital School.

Daniella Rotimi is the policy officer for Allergy UK, supporting the proposed solutions to some of the biggest issues facing the allergic community as well as publicising the resources and services Allergy UK has available.

James Shryane is headteacher at Hospital and Outreach Education AP Academy in Northamptonshire, part of the Skylark Partnership Trust, with responsibility for teaching children in hospitals, in outreach centres and in homes across the county. Prior to this he was assistant headteacher at

Oxfordshire Hospital School and spent 21 years working in secondary comprehensive schools. James holds a Master's Degree in Educational Leadership.

Rajwant Kaur Singh is the CEO of the Children's Heart Federation charity supported by a brilliant board, building new networks with businesses and seeking support to champion and support children with heart conditions and their families. Rajwant is the figurehead to fight the corner for children with heart conditions to make positive changes now, and for generations to come.

Penny White is an experienced educationalist and the deputy headteacher at Hospital and Outreach Education medical PRU. A qualified SENCO and experienced safeguarding lead, she has responsibility for the AV1 programme in the county and is passionate about the difference they make to learners. Penny currently works in Northamptonshire and leading on the AV1 programme in the county on behalf of the medical AP academy.

Chelsea Wong is the Young People and Family Support Officer for LUPUS UK, supporting the community of learners with lupus. She has lived with lupus since 2014 and understands the added challenges of living with an autoimmune condition to childhood. The charity wishes to support others within the community and amplify their voices.

Introduction
The purpose of this book and how you might use it

Cath Kitchen

Supporting learners with medical conditions in schools is an important part of inclusion, not only for their academic success but also for their well-being, social inclusion, and sense of belonging. You will increasingly be encountering learners with a diverse range of medical needs, yet you and the staff within your school may lack the specialized knowledge and resources to provide comprehensive support to enable these learners to thrive and be successful in their learning.

The underpinning principles running through this book are:

Ensuring equal access to education so learners with medical conditions can access the same educational opportunities as their peers. This book can help you identify practical tips and strategies for creating safe, inclusive, and accessible environments, and minimising barriers to learning.

Promoting physical and emotional well-being as learners with medical conditions may face additional stressors and anxieties that can impact their physical and mental health. Being able to attend a supportive school, feeling a sense of connection to their peers and the school community is often an important part of their treatment and recovery plans.

Legal compliance and your duty of care as you have a legal responsibility to safeguard the health and safety of all your learners, which includes managing medical conditions effectively and ensuring staff are prepared to respond appropriately. You will find details of your relevant legal obligations in this book, which will help you to avoid legal pitfalls and fulfil your duty of care with more confidence.

Building staff confidence and skills as often this is an area where accessing any training and support is a challenge, leaving staff feeling uncertain about handling learners' medical needs effectively. This book offers

DOI: 10.4324/9781003478942-1

some support, guidance, and reassurance which, when combined with advice from qualified medical practitioners, can help equip staff with the knowledge and skills to respond more confidently.

Supporting home-school partnerships as these strong, collaborative relationships between you and families are vital for effectively managing learners' medical needs in school. This book provides top tips and guidance on effective communication, to help you engage with families and health-care providers to build trust and ensure that each learner's individual needs are met.

Creating frameworks for best practices in your setting as schools can vary widely in their experience and capacity to support learners with medical needs. Although not a definitive guide, this book will give some suggestions on how to develop a clear framework of best practices that best meets the needs of your setting.

Promoting social inclusion and reducing stigma as learners with medical conditions can often feel isolated, stigmatised, and that they do not belong in their home school communities. This book will help to raise staff awareness about the impact of having a medical condition, promoting understanding and empathy, creating a more inclusive school environment where every learner feels valued and supported.

What learners are telling us . . .

In some recent research, learners with complex health conditions identified six key asks for their education:

- to safely manage my health at school
- a flexible education pathway
- to be acknowledged and listened to in the right way
- to be included in and supported by my school community
- to build towards my future
- to develop attitudes and approaches to support my emotional and mental health in school

All schools, including yours, want to be inclusive and ensure that these learners have their needs considered so they are enabled to flourish and thrive educationally, socially, and emotionally, and this book is designed to support you in this endeavour.

There are an increasing number of learners in mainstream schools with complex medical conditions, either those that were born with conditions, such as epilepsy, or those who have succumbed to them, such as cancer. Consequently, there are more children who need to be included in the life of your school, with ever diminishing access to resources, both human and financial.

The purpose of this book

This book is designed to provide you with an accessible, easy-access guide to providing the best possible support you can to your learners with medical needs who attend your school, enabling them to thrive and succeed.

Each chapter has background information, supporting case studies, and some 'top tips' for you to use, alongside reflective questions for you to con-sider about your practice.

You do not need to read this book from cover to cover. It is designed to be a 'dip in' resource, where you can access specific advice and resources to support you in including children in certain situations e.g. a child being admitted to hospital for cancer treatment. The chapters have been written by a wide range of practitioners who are experienced in their field of sup-porting children with medical conditions, who have shared their preferred approaches and practical strategies which have been tried and tested. We have consulted with school staff as to what they would like to know more about, and the response was a resounding endorsement for first-hand knowl-edge and experience to support children with medical needs in one place.

Sections of the book

Section 1 of the book, Chapters 1 to 3, sets out the legal framework and statutory responsibilities of schools to support learners with medical needs which sets the context. Chapter 4 outlines what you should expect from your Local Authority in terms of support and what they should be providing under their statutory duties.

Section 2 contains best practice examples of how to include children with medical needs in your school. This section has been authored by a variety of practitioners who have shared their knowledge and experiences as to what has worked with learners they have supported and will hopefully provide you with practical examples that you can use. This section includes a chapter written by a pharmacist on best practice in managing medication, which I know is often an area of concern for schools.

Section 3 looks at specific provisions and gives you an insight into how education is provided whilst learners are inpatients, and how you can collaborate and communicate effectively with hospital education teams to ensure continuity of the learner's education and smooth transition back to school.

Section 4 examines the next steps you could take and includes contributions from a range of children's health charities, and various resources you can access to support you in including children with medical needs. This also includes an audit tool you could use to assess your current position and look to how you can develop and improve your support.

By following the instructions at the front of this book, you will be able to access an array of useful online resources, including specimen polices, exemplar Individual Healthcare Plans, training materials for colleagues and governors, as well as some that have been generously shared by contributors.

We hope this book will be an invaluable resource, addressing a gap in current educational resources for this cohort of learners. We hope it will empower you and your school to uphold your commitment to every learner's inclusion and educational success, contributing to a culture where all your learners can thrive, regardless of their medical challenges.

"As the mother of a child who had complex medical difficulties which prevented her from attending school full time, I am passionate about ensuring that these learners, who are often quiet and not problematic, have access to the same high-quality education as their peers. Being ill is bad enough without a double whammy of getting behind and doing poorly at school".

Cath Kitchen

Bibliography

Spencer, B.K.C., Hugh-Jones, S., Cottrell, D. & Pini, S. (2023). *The INSCHOOL project: Young people with long-term physical health conditions: An in-depth qualitative study of their needs at school.* Journal of Adolescence, 96(2), pp. 337–349, accessed at https://onlinelibrary. wiley.com/doi/full/10.1002/jad.12278

SECTION 1
The legal bit

2

The legal requirements

Cath Kitchen

Introduction

The responsibilities of schools to support learners with medical conditions is outlined in the Department for Education (DfE) statutory guidance 'Supporting pupils with medical conditions at school', first produced in 2014, then updated in 2017. Like much of the government guidance currently, there is a combination of 'musts' (statutory) and 'shoulds' (best practice), and this chapter is going to unpick some of the details in the guidance.

The legislation itself is issued under Section 100 of the Children and Families Act that places a duty on governing bodies of maintained schools, proprietors of academies, and management committees of Pupil Referral Units (referred to in this chapter as governing bodies) to make arrangements for supporting learners with medical conditions at their school. It is also designed to assist and guide schools, academies and PRUs, local authorities, clinical commissioning groups and health service providers, parents/carers of children, and anyone who has an interest in promoting the well-being and academic attainment of learners with medical conditions. This includes independent schools.

The overall aim of the guidance is to ensure that all learners with medical conditions, in terms of both physical and mental health, are appropriately supported in school so that they can play a full and active role in school life, remain healthy, and achieve their academic potential. Parents also need to feel confident that the school will provide effective support for their child's medical condition and that they will be safe. Open and transparent communication and collaboration between all stakeholders is essential to the successful inclusion of a learner with medical conditions.

DOI: 10.4324/9781003478942-3

The role of governing bodies

Governing bodies are legally responsible and accountable for this statutory duty and must ensure that arrangements are in place so learners with medical conditions can access and enjoy the same opportunities in school as any other child. The focus of the arrangements should be on the needs of the individual child and how their medical condition impacts on their school life. Any plans will need to be flexible and responsive to those individual needs and give parents the confidence in the school's ability to provide effective support for their child. This will include any training needs for specific staff involved in the care of the learner.

Although all learners are entitled to full-time education, the nature of a learner's medical condition may require flexibility in that they may need arrangements for a part-time timetable. Putting a learner's health at risk in the case of an outbreak of an infectious disease in the school also needs to be considered. This is permissible and would be seen as a reasonable adjustment, included as part of an Individual Healthcare Plan (IHCP). More information on these plans can be found in Chapter 3.

Any policies, plans, procedures, and systems put in place need to be monitored and effectively implemented. It is good practice to have a governor on the board with a responsibility for oversight of provision for learners with medical conditions. This is often the SEND link governor.

There is a presentation that can be edited for governors on the role of the governing body in supporting learners with medical needs in the online resources section. There is also information on the National Governance Association website https://www.nga.org.uk/knowledge-centre/supporting-learners-with-medical-conditions/. This also contains a checklist for your school policy.

Governors should ensure that an appropriate level of insurance is in place that reflects the level of risk. It would be appropriate to include this in your policy.

Developing your school policy

The governing body is responsible for ensuring that your school develops a policy for supporting learners with medical conditions and, like other school policies, that this policy is reviewed annually and made accessible to all stakeholders, including parents. Best practice is to display this policy on your school website.

There should be a named person who has overall responsibility for the implementation of the policy, which needs to be someone in the school e.g. the Special Needs Coordinator or a senior leader. Collaboration with healthcare professionals, including the school nurse, can support the policy development and identify any training requirements for staff. There is an exemplar policy in the resources section.

Your policy should contain the following (most of this information can be found within the guidance):

- Named person responsible for making the arrangements for learners with medical conditions, ensuring staff are appropriately trained and that all staff are made aware of the learner's condition. This may include whole staff awareness training (note: a first aid certificate does not constitute appropriate training)
- Roles and responsibilities of key staff
- Cover arrangements in case of staff absence or turnover to ensure safety of the learner and that someone is always available
- Briefing for any cover teachers
- Procedures to follow when you are notified that a learner has a medical condition or if a learner with a medical condition is joining your school
- Any considerations of home-to-school transport
- How you will use the IHCPs, who will take responsibility for developing them, and how they will be monitored and updated
- How you will conduct risk assessments for external trips and visits and other activities outside the normal timetable, ensuring learners with medical conditions are included as far as possible
- Any additional measures you may put in place to minimise risks e.g. installation of a defibrillator, holding of asthma inhaler and adrenaline auto-injectors (may also be known as EpiPens) for emergency use
- Arrangements for learners who are competent to manage their own health needs and medication
- Procedures for dealing with emergency situations, and how you will develop and rehearse any emergency responses e.g. to severe allergic reactions, asthma attacks, or seizures

- Procedures for managing medicines (this may be contained in a separate 'Administration of Medication' policy – more information can be found in Chapter 12)
- What the school considers to be unacceptable practice and how you will manage complaints.

Roles and responsibilities of school staff and other stakeholders

- Headteachers should ensure that the policy is developed and implemented, and all staff are aware of their role within the policy. They are also responsible for ensuring that staff are appropriately trained, that appropriate IHCPs are in place, and that the school nurse is aware of any learners with medical conditions in the school.
- Parents should provide the school with up-to-date information about their child's medical needs and notify them of any changes in their condition. Parents are key partners in the development and review of IHCPs and take responsibility for any part of the plan that they have agreed to implement e.g. provision of medication and equipment, ensuring that they or another nominated adult are always contactable.
- Learners with medical conditions are often the best people to provide information about how their condition affects them. They should be fully involved in discussions related to the development of the IHCP and their role in implementation of the plan.
- School staff can be asked to provide support for learners with medical conditions, but they cannot be required to do so. They should receive sufficient and suitable training and acquire the necessary level of competence before they take on any support responsibilities. However, all staff should know what to do in an emergency, where a learner with medical needs requires help.
- School nurses can also notify schools when a child has been identified as having a medical condition, preferably before the child starts school. They may support staff in developing and implementing IHCP and provide advice and liaison on appropriate training to access. School nurses can consult with lead clinicians locally on appropriate support strategies,

and community and specialist nursing teams may also be a valuable resource for seeking advice for learners with specific medical conditions.

- Other healthcare professionals, such as GPs and paediatricians, will contact the school nurse about any child identified as having a medical condition that will need to be appropriately supported in school. They may also provide advice on developing IHCPs, and local specialist teams can provide support for schools in including learners with particular conditions e.g. diabetes, epilepsy.
- Local authorities are commissioners of school nurses and have a duty to provide cooperation between relevant partners with a view to improving the well-being of learners regarding their physical and mental health, their education, training, and recreation. More details on the role of local authorities can be found in Chapter 4.
- Integrated Care Boards (called Clinical Commissioning Groups in the guidance) came into existence in 2022. They are responsible for ensuring that commissioning is responsive to learner's needs and must make joint arrangements for education, health, and care provision for learners with SEN or disabilities.
- Providers of health services should also cooperate with schools who are supporting learners with medical conditions and can provide the outreach training and liaison with school, specialist, and community nursing teams. They can provide valuable support, information, and guidance to schools and staff, building confidence.
- Ofsted will consider how well the school meets the needs of the full range of learners, which will include those with medical conditions. Case studies about your approaches, including IHCPs, can be helpful to illustrate your practice.

What to do when you find out a learner has a medical condition

Many learners are born with medical conditions, so you will have information from their parents and, if appropriate, their previous educational settings. These learners may already have an IHCP in place, and you would review that on entry to your school with all the relevant healthcare professionals, the parent, and the learner if they have the required level of comprehension. Suitable transition arrangements, which may include additional taster days, a planned reintegration programme, individual sessions with key staff, etc. should be discussed and implemented in a timely manner.

However, some learners will become unwell once they are already on roll at your school. Do not wait for a formal diagnosis but start to consider how you can support the learner to be able to participate fully in school life. If a formal diagnosis is made, then the same planning processes would apply, including developing an IHCP (see Chapter 3).

The child's role in managing their own medical needs

In discussion with parents and the child, learners who are competent should be supported and encouraged to take responsibility for managing their own medicines and procedures. The arrangements for this would be clearly laid out in the IHCP.

If possible, learners can carry their own medicines and devices so that they can easily access them when required. Some may still need a level of supervision, and if they feel that they cannot manage, then relevant staff should be available to manage procedures for them.

Some learners, although competent, may not want to manage their own medicines. Staff should not force them, and alternative options should be documented on the IHCP.

Administering medicines at school (see also Chapter 12)

Your schools must have an administration of medicines policy, and it may sit within your health and safety policy. Below is a checklist of key points you need to ensure are included:

- Only administer medicines at school when it would be detrimental to a child's health or attendance not to do so.
- Do not give any child under 16 any prescription or non-prescription medicines without their parent's written consent.

- Only accept prescribed medicines that are in-date, labelled, provided in the original container as dispensed by a pharmacist, and include instructions for administration, dosage, and storage. The exception to this is insulin, which must be in date, but may be supplied in a pen or pump rather than the original container.
- Clearly set out the circumstances in which non-prescription medicines may be administered. If administering medication e.g. for pain relief, check the maximum dosage, when the last dose was given, and inform the parents.
- No child under 16 should be given medicines containing aspirin unless prescribed by a doctor.
- Where clinically possible, medicines should be prescribed in dose frequency which enables them to be taken outside school hours.
- Detail how the medicines will be stored safely and how learners will know where they are and how to access them immediately.
- Detail how medicines such as asthma inhalers, blood glucose testing kits, and adrenaline auto-injector pens will not be locked away, but will be more readily available to learners.
- Detail any arrangements that will need to be made as part of a risk assessment for any external trip or visit or emergency.
- Detail how you will keep written records of all medicines administered to learners.

Sensitivity and confidentiality

Many learners with medical conditions are sensitive about being different to their peers and may be embarrassed by any singling out or being made to feel different. Discuss this with the child and their parents and ask them what they would like you to do. Some like you to tell their class/peer group/year group so that they are aware, and this approach often encourages empathy and understanding for the child. This supports an inclusive environment for all learners, regardless of their health condition.

Any information relating to the child's medical condition will be private and needs to be appropriately stored and shared as permitted under the General Data Protection Regulations, and appropriate permissions may need to be sought.

Self-reflection

Does your school have a policy? Review the policy and consider if it fulfils all the requirements. Has it been discussed with the school nurse?

Is there a named governor for learners with medical needs? Seek them out and introduce yourself, talk to them about the policy.

Could you convene a representative group of learners in the school who have medical conditions or members of the school council to discuss the policy so you can include their input?

5 top tips

1. Develop a robust policy that is owned by the governors and appoint a link governor.
2. Carry out a whole school audit to check you are legally compliant and using best practice to support learners with medical conditions (see resources).
3. Ensure you access the appropriate training to be able to support the child in school.
4. Consult with all stakeholders so there is joint responsibility, including the child and their parents.
5. Be sensitive and empathetic to both the child and the parent – having a medical condition that requires special arrangements and medication is a challenge for them!

Note: there will be training presentations for all stakeholders in the resources for stakeholders, along with exemplar plans and templates.

Reference

Department for Education (2017). *Supporting learners with medical conditions at school.* Accessed 14.05.24 at https://www.gov.uk/government/publications/supporting-pupils-at-school-with-medical-conditions--3

3

Individual Healthcare Plans

Cath Kitchen

Introduction

Individual Healthcare Plans (IHCPs) are useful documents for ensuring that learners with medical needs can thrive in schools with all their needs being appropriately accommodated. They are hugely underused and need to be prioritised as part of your overall SEND provision and support.

What is an Individual Healthcare Plan (IHCP)?

An Individual Healthcare Plan (IHCP) is used in education settings to detail exactly what sort of care a learner may need at school if they have a medical condition. Individual Healthcare Plans do not have to be created for every learner and are usually only used for learners with medical conditions that:

- are long-term and complex;
- may fluctuate;
- are a recurring condition; or
- where there is an elevated risk that emergency intervention will be required.

The decision as to whether a learner requires one falls to the headteacher.

You do not need to wait for a formal diagnosis by a medical practitioner before putting an IHCP in place to provide support for learners, as early

DOI: 10.4324/9781003478942-4

intervention with the right support can enable the learner to continue to attend school successfully. If the condition and its impact on the learner is unclear, the headteacher will make a judgement about what support to provide to the learner, based on medical evidence available at the time that the school is made aware of an issue. The headteacher will consider the views of the learner and their parents, alongside any available medical evidence, but is entitled to challenge the evidence if appropriate.

The aim of an IHCP is to ensure that schools know how best to support the learner effectively and to provide clarity about what needs to be done, when, and by whom so the learner is enabled to thrive in school, ensuring that they have access to the same opportunities as their peers.

IHCPs should always be devised with the learner's best interest in mind, with the desired outcome for them to be able to enjoy school and access the same opportunities as their peers. Each learner needs to be treated as an individual, as every learner copes differently with various medical conditions; you cannot make assumptions that e.g. if a learner has diabetes, then their IHCP will be identical to another learner who has the same condition.

In some cases, depending on the learner, their age, and various other attributes, learners will want to manage their own medical needs, and this should be documented on the IHCP. For example, each learner should be assessed, and the IHCP will document whether the learner carries their own medication to administer themselves and whether they wish to do so.

Who should be involved in developing an IHCP?

IHCPs are developed in partnership between the school, parents, learners, and the relevant healthcare professional who can advise on a learner's case. There is an exemplar letter for you to invite parents into school to develop the plan, with an explanation of what an IHCP is and what it is used for, on the Department for Education (DfE) website. Plans should be kept confidential but easily accessible and shared with school staff and other professionals who may need to be aware of the learner's medical condition.

The school is responsible for making and writing the plan.

The headteacher is responsible for:

- Overseeing the plan development (they do not need to be directly involved)
- Ensuring all relevant staff who need to know about the plan are aware of it
- Ensuring that staff are appropriately insured to support learners with their medical needs
- Ensuring that there are enough trained staff available to implement the plan, including in contingency and emergency situation arrangements.

Parents are responsible for:

- Informing the school what exactly their learner's medical needs are, and sharing any advice and guidance from any healthcare practitioners their learner may have seen
- Updating the school immediately if anything changes
- Carrying out actions they have agreed to do as part of the IHCP e.g. providing medicines and equipment or ensuring they or another nominated adult are always contactable.

Learners should:

- Be involved in any discussions about their health needs, including explaining how they feel their medical condition impacts on them in school
- Have input and contribute to their plan
- Follow the processes and arrangements set out in their plan.

Healthcare professionals e.g. the school nurse or the learner's paediatrician should:

- Provide advice on how a learner's medical needs can be met in the school environment
- Support the school with additional advice when needed
- Support learners with specific medical conditions such as diabetes and epilepsy: this may be from specialist local health teams.

What should an IHCP include?

There are various templates available to guide you in devising and developing your IHCPs (see resources section) including one from the DfE and many exemplars from the charities that support learners with different health conditions (see Chapter 16), so you do not need to start from nothing.

An IHCP should include:

- Learner's details – name, address, DOB, class
- Medical diagnosis or condition
- Family contact information – names, contact numbers, address, relationship to the learner
- GP and hospital contact numbers and names
- The person responsible for providing support in school (may be multiple people)
- Description of medical needs and details of learner's symptoms, triggers, signs, treatments, facilities, equipment or devices, etc.
- Precisely what help the learner needs to manage their condition, what they can do themselves, and what they need from another (including supervision)
- Consider environmental issues of being in school such as crowded corridors, travel time between lessons, noisy classrooms, carrying books/ bags, etc.
- Name(s) of medication, dose, method of administration, when to be taken, side effects, contra-indications, administered by/self-administered with/without supervision
- Daily care requirements – including what medication they require during the school day and any dietary needs, etc.
- If a learner has special educational needs, but does not have an Education, Health and Care Plan (EHCP), their SEN needs should be mentioned in the IHCP
- Where a learner has a Statement of Special Educational Needs (SEN) or an EHCP, how the Individual Healthcare Plan should be linked to or become part of that Statement or Plan
- Any specific support for the learner's educational, personal, social, and emotional needs e.g. staying in at break time, access to the school counsellor, catch up sessions, etc.

- Any plans and special arrangements that need to be put in place for exams (if appropriate)
- Any specific arrangements for school trips and visits (please note you would also undertake a risk assessment in preparation for any trips and visits)
- What constitutes a medical emergency – what action to take, who to contact
- Details of people involved in the development of the plan
- How to manage queries about confidentiality and when those rules can be breached e.g. in the case of an emergency
- Date of when the plan was created and when it will be next reviewed
- Any additional staff training required to appropriately support the learner e.g. EpiPen training
- Any other useful information – no information is bad information.

You will also need a separate document with the written permission from parents and the headteacher for medication to be administered by a member of staff, or self-administered by the learner, and recording any administration of medication (see Chapter 12).

What is the process to develop the IHCP?

The development of the IHCP is a useful tool to get all relevant people involved in the learner's care discussing solutions and adjustments collectively. The actual template and information you need to collect forms a useful agenda for the meeting, which should always be focussed on the needs of the learner and enabling them to thrive in your school.

Below are some guidance steps you could use to help you:

1. Gather initial information – a parent or healthcare professional informs you that one of your learners

   - has been newly diagnosed
   - is due to start at your school
   - is due to return to school after a long-term absence (which could include a hospital inpatient stay).
   - or that the learner's medical needs have changed.

2. Invite parents to a meeting to discuss the learner's medical support needs – this may be coordinated by the headteacher or a senior member of school staff who will also identify key school staff who will provide any additional support needed. At this meeting, a decision will be made as to whether an IHCP is required (please note for ALL complex health conditions, an IHCP is required).
3. Invite key stakeholders to a meeting to discuss and develop the IHCP. This should include key school staff, the learner, parent, relevant health-care professional, and other medical/health clinician as appropriate (or you can consider written evidence provided by them).
4. Develop the IHCP in partnership, where input from a healthcare profes-sional MUST be provided. The school needs to take the lead on writing and disseminating it, including giving a copy to the parent and learner (if appropriate).
5. Identify any additional staff training needs and arrange for this to take place.
6. Implement the IHCP, circulate and inform all relevant staff, and make other staff aware of where the plan is stored for emergency purposes.
7. Set a date to review the plan, at least annually, but best practice is termly.

Reviewing IHCPs

IHCPs should be reviewed at least annually, though it is best practice to review them at least once a term, as medical conditions can fluctuate and change. If circumstances do change, the parent or healthcare professional may ask the school to review the plan. Reviews should always involve the parent and the learner (if appropriate), relevant school staff, and health professionals involved in the learner's care. School nurses are often involved too (see above).

Transition between schools

Like learners with identified SEND needs, details about a learner's medical condition and their current IHCP must be shared with the new school or post-16 destination. It is best practice for the parent, the learner, their current school, and the new setting to meet, along with any relevant healthcare professionals to ensure that appropriate plans are put in place. Note that there is no statutory requirement for post-16 settings to have IHCPs in place, but it is certainly helpful for them to have one!

Self-reflection

- Consider your own role in compiling IHCPs – do you feel confident you have the skills and knowledge to produce a useful document? Are you using the expertise of the school nurse? Do you know where to seek additional support if you need it?
- Have you looked at the exemplars on the children's health charity websites to support you? It is worth making time to do this before you start!

5 top tips

1. ALL learners with complex health conditions should have an IHCP.
2. Remember that the parent and the learner are experts in their knowledge about their medical condition and how it impacts them.
3. Make sure that healthcare professionals participate in the development of the plan.
4. Review the plan when required.
5. Make sure all staff know what a helpful document the IHCP is, and how they can make best use of it to enable the learner to thrive.

Bibliography

Department for Education (2017). *Supporting pupils with medical conditions at school: Templates*. Accessed 14.05.24 at https://www.gov.uk/government/publications/supporting-pupils-at-school-with-medical-conditions--3

4

Local authority (LA) responsibilities

Cath Kitchen

Introduction

This chapter will outline the statutory guidance for local authorities (LAs), their responsibilities, and how these link with the school's responsibilities. This will include policies that should be available and how schools should work collaboratively with their LA to meet their learner's medical needs.

What are the statutory responsibilities of the LA?

As well as schools, LAs also have a responsibility for arranging education for learners who cannot attend school because of health needs. These responsibilities are laid out in statutory guidance of the same name, 'Arranging education for children who cannot attend school because of health needs' (December 2023) (see resources), and relate to LA statutory duties under Section 19 of the Education Act 1966.

The Section 19 duty states that LAs are responsible for arranging suitable and (normally) full-time education for learners of compulsory school age who, because of exclusion, illness, or other reasons, would not receive suitable education without such provision.

All LAs should have a written, publicly accessible policy statement on their arrangements for complying with the Section 19 duty. The policy should link to related services in the area, for example: special educational needs

DOI: 10.4324/9781003478942-5

and disability (SEND) services, child and adolescent mental health services (CAMHS), education welfare and attendance improvement services, educational psychologists, and school nurses, where relevant.

Your LA should have a named officer who is responsible for the education of learners with health needs.

When does the LA need to become involved in the education of learners with medical needs?

Where possible, a learner's health needs should be managed by your school so that they can continue to be educated there with support, and without the need for the intervention of the LA. The LA does not need to become involved in such arrangements unless it has reason to believe that the education being provided by you is unsuitable.

However, as soon as you can no longer support their health needs and provide suitable education, you should speak to your LA about putting alternative provision/arrangements in place.

You should find out what arrangements your LA has for providing education for learners with medical needs under their Section 19 duty, as there are different ways that they can arrange education. This may be through a hospital school, a medical alternative provision, a specialist academy, a home tuition service, online learning provision (either in-house or externally commissioned) or, if appropriate, through an unregistered alternative provision.

Your role when your learner is referred to alternative provision

Your learner will remain dual registered with you whilst they attend the alternative provision, and you are the main school. You will need to liaise closely with the AP, provide appropriate work, and attend regular review meetings.

If your learner is taking external examinations, you may need to make the exam arrangements and any other access arrangements.

Your role in supporting your learner when they are admitted to hospital for an inpatient stay

See Chapters 14 and 15 for how best to support learners who are admitted for a hospital inpatient stay.

Your role in supporting your learner when they are ready to return to school

When your learner is ready to return to school, you will work closely with the AP provider to compose a sustainable plan. As you have already been providing the same work and curriculum resources as the learner's peers are using, alongside ensuring that the learner still feels connected to their teachers and peers and that they belong in school, this should be more straightforward. You may decide to use an IHCP as a reintegration plan.

Further details about reintegration practice can be found in Chapter 13.

Collaborating with parents and carers

It is good practice for you, the LA, the learner, and parents/carers to work closely together when considering arrangements for a learner who is too unwell to attend school and who requires alternative provision. Parents/carers (and, where appropriate, the learner themselves) have a key role to play and can provide essential information about the learner and their needs and should always be consulted before new provision begins. Likewise, parents/carers and the learner should be consulted at any change-points in the learner's provision as well as when they are ready to reintegrate back into your school.

Self-reflection

- Are you including all relevant stakeholders in your discussions about arrangements for learners with medical needs who might need to access alternative provision or who are going into hospital? Parents/carers and learners are the most important people to include and listen to.

5 top tips

1. Check out your LA Policy for Children with Medical Needs and the named responsible officer.
2. Check out the arrangements under Section 19 for learners with medical needs in your local authority, and to whom you would make a referral.
3. Collaborate closely with parents/carers and learners (where appropriate) and ensure you value and respect their views.
4. Collaborate closely with the alternative provider in partnership to ensure the best possible outcomes for your learner.
5. Welcome your learner back to school when they are ready.

Reference

Department for Education (2023). *Arranging education for children who cannot attend school because of health needs.* Crown Copyright. Accessed 28.10.24 at https://assets.publishing.service.gov.uk/media/657995f0254aaa000d050bff/Arranging_education_for_children_who_cannot_attend_school_because_of_health_needs.pdf

SECTION 2

Best practice examples of how to include learners with medical needs in your school

Checking for dragons and potholes

Creating a welcoming environment for learners with medical conditions

Tara Bell

Introduction

This chapter examines various 'dragons' (active harms) and 'potholes' (unintended effects) in schools that impact upon vulnerable learners, particularly those experiencing or recovering from medical illnesses. These preventable harms can emerge in the most well-intentioned and well-informed school environment. The chapter explores solutions from leadership and culture to communication, quality of education, and considerations for behaviour and neurodiversity.

In the wake of the COVID-19 pandemic, there was a strong push for change within schools (e.g., Brighouse and Waters, 2021; NEU, 2020; NAHT, 2021; Vegas and Winthrop, 2020). Schools recognised the trauma experienced by learners and families, leading to curriculum adjustments and increased focus on well-being (Fotheringham et al., 2021). However, by 2022, many schools reverted to pre-pandemic norms, missing an opportunity for lasting change. For learners with medical needs, the temporary adjustments seen during the pandemic should serve as a model for ongoing care and consideration.

This chapter draws on literature, individual experiences, and insights from staff and learners. Learners' words are anonymised and come from a 2022 questionnaire on school experiences during illness. Staff perspectives (M and S) are from a 2024 interview with hospital teaching staff on supporting learners reintegrating into mainstream schools.

Leadership and culture

Schools are complex organisations that demand clear policies and systems to function effectively. However, rigid enforcement can disproportionately affect the most vulnerable learners, including those with medical conditions.

For learners grappling with mental or physical health challenges, the capacity of their school to adapt its rules, provide support, and offer understanding can be pivotal to their success. Schools that strike a balance between flexibility, patience, and maintaining ambitious standards are likely to see fewer instances of absenteeism, learner departures to alternative provision, choosing home education, or disruptions due to health-related issues.

In M's experience as a hospital teacher supporting mainstream schools, she noted that effective leadership teams in mainstream schools understand that progress may not always follow a linear path. These leaders prioritise being actively involved in the lives of vulnerable learners, taking the time to connect with them, showing genuine curiosity about their needs. This visible care not only fosters a sense of belonging among these learners, but also raises their visibility among the broader staff group.

Embracing a leadership approach that prioritises empathy, understanding, and proactive support for vulnerable learners creates an environment where all learners feel valued.

Self-reflection

- Do leaders in your school play a crucial role in shaping the climate and setting the tone in the school?
- Do leaders actively seek out vulnerable or unwell learners, listen to their needs, and empower their teams to find solutions?

Welcoming learners back to school: Communication and relationships

Preparation, people, and places

Re-entering school after an illness can present significant challenges due to the effects of treatment, absence, poor peer relationships, and insufficient preparation and communication between schools, families, and clinicians.

Effective reintegration involves comprehensive planning and consideration of several key factors which can prevent setbacks and support a smooth transition (see also Chapter 13):

- Creation of an Individual Healthcare Plan with input from parents and clinicians, centred on the learner's and family's voices (see Chapter 3).
- Identified trusted adults and safe spaces within school to provide consistent support and a secure environment.
- Detailed, co-produced reintegration plan with clear timings, school map, and locations for start and end of the day, and transitions, including a peer buddy system.
- Agreed communication tools such as time-out cards, RAG notices, and symbols or objects to communicate needs are established to prevent setbacks.

Self-reflection

- Is the school entrance the learners are required to use public and accessible, and comfortable for them?
- Do you provide training for administrative staff so they can appropriately welcome returning learners and flag individual triggers to support the learner effectively?
- Do you inform teaching staff of the returning learner's needs, promote a trauma-informed approach, and ensure interactions are warm and clear to support successful reintegration?
- Do you have a truly 'safe space' for learners with varying needs?

Communication and relationships

Learners with medical needs and their families often experience trauma, making effective communication crucial (Wilcox et al., 2016; Cabizuca et al., 2009). Schools must ensure that all communication, whether through documentation, meetings, displays, or everyday interactions, is clear, empathetic, and supportive.

Areas to consider when supporting learners include:

- Adopting a trauma-informed approach, always starting with empathy and validation, considering facial expressions, tone, body language, and terminology.
- Kindness should be the primary response, with reprimands and sanctions as a secondary disappointing reaction if necessary.
- Positively acknowledge efforts using welcoming phrases like "I'm so thrilled you're with us for this piece of work" to refocus on learning. Try to avoid sarcastic remarks like "oh, you've graced us with your presence," which can create barriers.
- Regular, warm greetings and check-ins are vital. For example, ensuring a learner is greeted each morning, as S highlighted in our discussions, prevents feelings of neglect and promotes a sense of belonging. M emphasised the importance of showing learners that they are in your thoughts even when they are not in school. Simple gestures like sending a message or note can make a profound difference in creating a sense of belonging.
- Consider the role of pastoral or form tutors, stressing the need for allocating more time for pastoral care thereby enabling meaningful interactions.
- Provide staff with training in building relationships and helping learners form connections with peers.

Areas to consider for supporting families:

- Acknowledge that parents may also experience Post Traumatic Stress Disorder following their child's illness (Woolf et al., 2016). Effective communication with parents can alleviate their fears and build trust.

- Prioritise effective communication where simple gestures, such as texts updating parents on their child's progress, can significantly reduce anxiety and reinforce trust in the school.

Self-reflection

- Do you prioritise strong supportive relationships with learners and families so that they feel valued and included, particularly when returning after a period of illness?

Quality of education

In the aftermath of widespread illness and trauma, the 'Recovery Curriculum' (2021) shifted focus from purely academic catch-up to promoting socialisation, the arts, sports, and communal cultural events. However, the dominance of the English Baccalaureate (EBacc) in many schools over the past decade has created potential pitfalls, particularly for otherwise motivated and high-achieving learners. Research highlights several key points:

- The narrowing of curriculum choices negatively impacts student attainment, engagement, and well-being (House of Commons, 2018; Yu and Mocan, 2019).
- The offer of a broad curriculum including arts, vocational training, and physical education have positive effects on student outcomes (Hope, 2006; Biddle et al., 2019; Sobel, 2020; APPGAHW, 2017). However, there has been an erosion of these subjects in schools (BBC, 2019; Achtaridou et al., 2022; Neumann et al., 2016).
- While research supports the benefits of summative and formative testing for learning (Bangert-Drowns et al., 1991), there is insufficient evidence on the efficacy of high-stakes testing as an indicator of learner ability. High-stakes testing is also linked to negative impacts on student well-being, including increased rates of adolescent suicide in societies that emphasise such testing (Wang, 2016).

Self-reflection

- Does your school offer a diverse broad curriculum beyond the EBacc to engage all learners and support their well-being?
- Does your curriculum emphasise socialisation, the arts, sports, and cultural events to support recovery from trauma?
- Does your curriculum avoid narrowing and enable flexible curriculum choices to ensure all learners have access to subjects that interest and motivate them?
- Do you consider carefully how and where you deliver examinations, including how you can maximise use of each access arrangement, reasonable adjustment, and special consideration?

Behaviour, neurodiversity, and additional educational needs (AENs)

In hospital schools, particularly Tier 4 CAMHS Schools, teachers continue to encounter learners who report that they have been told by their mainstream school that it is not the right 'fit' for them. This situation arises due to resource constraints in schools and the pressure of accountability frameworks which often incentivise schools to avoid admitting disadvantaged learners, as these learners' outcomes might negatively impact the school's chances of achieving an 'outstanding' judgement (O'Brien, 2016).

Learners with medical (physical or mental) health needs are particularly affected by these systemic issues. The prevalent deficit outlook on disability and neurodiversity in education is perpetuated by terminology that reinforces negative perceptions, such as 'able' and 'not able.' Adopting growth mindset language can raise aspirations and improve well-being for all learners (Dweck, 2006). Schools are also caught between the growing complexity of learner needs and a system that prioritises narrow attainment metrics, which means that learners with medical needs may be marginalised.

To better support learners with additional needs, schools should:

- Adopt a growth mindset with a shift from a deficit outlook to one that emphasises potential and growth.
- Equip teaching staff with a range of behavioural and pedagogical strategies to meet diverse needs.
- Develop inclusive policies that accommodate the complexities of learners with medical and mental health needs, ensuring they can achieve ambitious standards in both behaviour and learning.

Self-reflection

- Do you ensure that resource constraints and accountability pressures do not push these vulnerable learners out of mainstream education?
- Do you avoid deficit terminology that labels learners as 'able' or 'not able, contributing to negative perceptions and outcomes?
- Can you adopt growth-oriented language and practices which can significantly enhance learner aspirations and well-being?
- Do you have/can you develop a broad toolkit of strategies to support the diverse pedagogical and emotional needs of learners with medical or mental health challenges?

Case study – Evie's story

Evie is a Year 9 learner who has significant mental health difficulties, following bullying at school and online. She exhibits self-harming behaviours and post-traumatic stress, but is well supported by her mother who provides a feeling of safety and frequently communicates with her by text.

When Evie came into school, she refused to give up her phone, and school viewed her refusal as a threat to safety within the school. She was consequently suspended.

When she returned to school after the suspension, the head of year met with Evie and her mum to listen to why Evie felt she needed to keep her phone with her, and they were able to explain that this was a coping mechanism for her to manage her mental health issues. A trusted adult was assigned to Evie to provide support if she felt she needed it, and Evie was given a part-time timetable initially to help reduce her stress and anxiety about bullying.

The time in school was gradually increased alongside support from the school counsellor on what other coping mechanisms/support she could access in school, which meant that she did not need to rely so heavily on always having her phone with her.

This case study illustrates that if you can tailor support plans to meet the unique needs of each learner, especially those with mental health challenges, you can work together to develop solutions. Adopting a compassionate, flexible approach to rule enforcement, prioritising the well-being of the learner is helpful, and using your network of support from other professionals, such as CAMHS workers, can support you in developing these plans.

Reflect on and learn from each case you come across to improve policies and practices, ensuring that you recognise and address potential pitfalls that could jeopardise a learner's future.

5 top tips

1. Ensure the leadership within your school is flexible and resilient so you can be adaptable, patient, and actively engaged with vulnerable learners.
2. Ensure all your communication is learner- and family-centred, which is both respectful and empathetic, fostering trust and supporting learner reintegration to school.
3. Create a welcoming environment to maintaining school attendance and preventing setbacks.
4. Offer a broad and diverse set of subjects beyond the Ebacc so all learners can engage and succeed.
5. Combining high behavioural standards with empathy through a trauma-informed approach will benefit all learners and support those with additional needs.

References

Achtaridou, E. et al. (2022). Department of Education. *School Recovery Strategies: Year 1 findings.* DoE. ISBN: 978-1-83870-324-0

All-Party Parliamentary Group on Arts, Health and Wellbeing Inquiry Report (APPGAHW). July 2017. *Creative health: The arts for health and wellbeing.* Culture Health and Wellbeing. Available at: https://www.culturehealthandwellbeing.org.uk/appg-inquiry. Accessed 01.03.22.

Bangert-Drowns, R.L., Kulik, J.A. & Kulik, C.-L.C. (1991). *Effects of frequent classroom testing,* Journal of Educational Research, 85(2), pp. 89–99. doi :10.1080/00220671.1991.10702818.

BBC News 8th March 2019. *Music lessons being stripped out of schools.* Available at https://www.bbc.co.uk/news/entertainment-arts-4748524002. Accessed 02.10.21.

Biddle, S.J.H. et al. (2019). *Physical activity and mental health in learners and adolescents: An updated review of reviews and an analysis of causality,* Psychology of Sport and Exercise, 42, pp. 146–155. Available at: https://doi.org/10.1016/j.psychsport.2018.08.011. Accessed 02.10.21.

Brighouse, T. & Waters, M. (2021). *About our schools: Improving on previous best.* Bancyfelin, Carmarthen: Crown House Publishing.

Cabizuca, M., Marques-Portella, C., Mendlowicz, M.V., Coutinho, E.S.F. & Figueira, I. (2009). *Posttraumatic stress disorder in parents of learners with chronic illnesses: A meta-analysis.* Health Psychology, 28(3), pp. 379–388.

Dweck, C. S. (2006). *Mindset: The new psychology of success.* Random House.

Fotheringham et al. (2021). *Pressures and influences on school leaders navigating policy development during the COVID-19 pandemic.* British Education Research Journal, 48(2), pp. 201–227.

Hope, T. (2006) *Are schools in tune with disaffected youth?* International Journal on School Disaffection, 4(2), pp. 28–34. Available at: https://doi.org/10.18546/ijsd.04.2.06.

House of Commons Report. Fifth Report of Session (2017–19). Released 2018. *Forgotten learners: Alternative provision and the scandal of ever-increasing exclusions.* Available: https://publications.parliament.uk/pa/cm201719/cmselect/cmeduc/342/342.pdf. Accessed 02.10.21.

Neumann et al., National Union of Teachers. (2016). *A curriculum for all? The effects of recent Key Stage 4 curriculum, assessment and accountability reforms on English secondary education.* Kings College London.

O'Brien, J. (2016). *Don't send him in tomorrow: Shining a light on the marginalised, disenfranchised and forgotten learners of today's schools.* Bancyfelin, Carmarthen, Wales: Independent Thinking Press.

Paton, M. NAHT (2021). *A time to recover.* Available at https://features.naht.org.uk/education_recovery/. Accessed 12.12.21.

Sobel, David. (2020). *School outdoors: The pursuit of happiness as an educational goal,* Journal of Philosophy of Education, 54(4), pp. 1064–1070. Available at: https://doi.org/10.1111/1467-9752.12458.

Vegas, E. & Winthrop, R. (2020). Brookings. 8th September 2020. *Beyond reopening schools: How education can emerge stronger than before COVID-19.* Available at https://www.brookings.edu/research/beyond-reopening-schools-how-education-can-emerge-stronger-than-before-covid-19/. Accessed: 10.10.20.

Wang, L. (2016). *The effect of high-stakes testing on suicidal ideation of teenagers with reference-dependent preferences,* Journal of Population Economics, 29(2), pp. 345–364. doi:10.1007/s00148-015-0575-7.

Wilcox, H. et al. (2016). *Behavioural problems and service utilization in learners with chronic illnesses referred for trauma-related mental health services.* Journal of Developmental & Behavioural Pediatrics, 37(1), pp. 62–70, January 2016. | DOI: 10.1097/DBP.0000000000000236

Woolf, C., Muscara, F., Anderson, V.A. & McCarthy, M.C. (2016). *Early traumatic stress responses in parents following a serious illness in their child: A systematic review.* J Clin Psychol Med Settings, 23, pp. 53–66. https://doi.org/10.1007/s10880-015-9430-y

Yu, H. & Mocan, N. (2019) *The impact of high school curriculum on confidence, academic success, and mental and physical well-being of university learners,* Journal of Labour Research, 40(4), pp. 428–462. doi:10.1007/s12122-019-09295-y.

6 Promoting and supporting attendance

Simon Pini and Vicky Hopwood

Introduction

This chapter focuses on how you can support learners with long-term physical health conditions (LTPHCs) to attend more regularly through accommodating their needs in your school and provides examples of practices and adjustments that you could consider. Using first-hand accounts gathered from 89 learners and 27 parents involved in the INSCHOOL research project, we describe ways you could support the attendance needs of learners with LTPHCs at your school.

Context

Estimates suggest there are around 1–1.7 million learners with medical conditions in the UK, which is about 10–17% of the school population and around 3 to 4 learners in every classroom. It is difficult to give exact figures as numbers often focus on specific conditions rather than the entire population of learners with LTPHCs. This figure of 1.7 million is probably an underestimation, and it is likely that there are a significant number of learners with LTPHCs in your school and classrooms who you are unaware of and whose needs are currently unmet.

Regardless of the medical condition – be that allergies, diabetes, cancer or colorectal conditions – we know from our research that there are shared challenges that learners with LTPHCs face in your school. Therefore, in developing approaches to support the inclusion of one learner with a LTPHC, you are likely to be putting in place strategies that are helpful for all.

DOI: 10.4324/9781003478942-8

Schools are increasingly being pressured to increase attendance, and there seems to be a relentless focus on attendance at all costs. However, learners with LTPHCs will inevitably miss school because of their ill health, medical appointments and because they have been recommended to stay at home, so tackling attendance for these learners is not simply about increasing the amount of time they spend in school. You need to consider providing for the broader holistic needs they face, as this is likely to be more helpful in addressing attendance than attendance rewards/incentives or punitively looking to increase attendance rates.

About the research

INSCHOOL is a large-scale research study capturing first-hand experiences of school life from learners with a diverse range of LTPHCs. It shows that everyday practices commonly adopted by schools to promote high attendance can be detrimental for this group of learners (Hopwood et al., 2024).

Learners taking part in the INSCHOOL study told us about their lives at school in their own words, and analysis of their stories revealed that all participants shared six common needs in school regardless of their specific health condition. These needs are often unmet and ultimately played an important part in their attendance at school (Hopwood et al., 2024; Spencer et al., 2023a; Spencer et al., 2023b). Addressing these six areas of need maximises opportunities for them to go to school and ensures appropriate strategies are in place for the times they cannot attend.

What do learners tell us about attending school with a medical condition?

Learners with LTPHCs value education and want to go to school; however, it is often not a choice of whether to attend or not. Sometimes they are too ill, or medical appointments are too inflexible or too far away to avoid missing school. Learners told us they schedule medical appointments and surgeries to minimise time away and try to avoid missing core lessons as they do not want to fall behind or miss school.

> *"If I feel like I can walk, then I'd definitely go to school, you don't want to miss important classes like English, maths." Age 13, Dermatology*
> *"After my big operation . . . literally like three days after my operation [I was] sat up in my bed doing maths or whatever." Age 15, Neuromuscular*
> *"Having to go to the hospital and have my appointment and then go into school, I was missing half a day at a time, so I was missing loads of lessons." Age 18, Chronic Pain*

These learners can be balancing competing health and education needs when attending school – meaning they may have to sacrifice one issue for the other. For some learners attending part-time is better for their recovery, but this may not be considered as an option.

They often feel unfairly treated because they cannot achieve attendance targets set for their class or the school, as reward schemes are not always effectively adjusted for their situations, setting high percentage targets which they are unable to achieve. This can also lead to marginalisation of the learner if their whole class misses a reward because of their attendance and the relationship with school has suffered due to needs not being addressed so school is not as welcoming as it could be.

> *"What really upsets me is when school has reward days if you've got over 97% and you're there and all the class has gone for pizza, and you're sat in the class and you're like 'it's not my fault'." Age 16, Chronic Pain*
> *"We get told our percentage . . . how much time we're in school, and people get awards for having good attendance . . . It's not so much that I'm being told that my attendance is bad and needs to be improved, but just more people are being congratulated for their good attendance where for me it's not something that can be helped . . . I happen to go to hospital sometimes . . . Then I miss out on awards [but] that is not a choice." Age 11, Cystic Fibrosis*

Some learners with LTPHC do not want to go to school – showing emotionally based school avoidance (EBSA) or disengagement from school. This may be because they are worried about going back to school after a long absence and are fearful about being behind, they may have been bullied and again, the relationship with school has suffered due to needs not being addressed so school are not as welcoming as they could be.

Self-reflection

- Could any of these quotes have come from learners in your school?
- Do you have any flexibility in the attendance targets that are set for learners with long-term complex health conditions?
- Is there anything you could do differently?

Common needs impacting attendance

Regardless of their condition, learners with LTPHCs have six common needs which were identified in the research as having an impact on their ability to attend school.

1. The need to safely manage their health at school
    This includes providing reasonable adjustments; help with managing symptoms, medication and treatment; and plans for when the learner is feeling unwell.

> *"I have a lift pass but like the teachers are always asking me if I actually do need one, and why I need it, because I look fit enough to walk up the stairs." Age 14, Diabetes*
> *"I couldn't trust them and didn't feel like safe, because I wanted to come home when I was in pain, but I wasn't allowed. So, I'd have to message my mum, which could get me in trouble." Age 16, Chronic Pain*

2. The need for a flexible education pathway
    This includes keeping/catching up with work; maintaining focus and managing the impact of their health condition during lessons; possibly reducing the number of subjects studied; and adjustments and plans for exams and revision are made promptly.

> *"At one point it was just a cycle of sleeping, school catching up, sleeping, school catching up, and it's just so continuous." Age 16, Chronic Pain*
> *"I just have to catch up by myself, like I'll ask my friends what we did in class and catch up by myself." Age 16, Allergies*

3. The need to be acknowledged and listened to in the right way
    This includes managing attention, comments and questions; concerns about visibility and appearance; wanting to be believed, listened to and understood; and the ability to control the narrative around their own medical condition.

> *"I think it's like the difference between wrong attention and right attention, like you want to inform people about it, but you don't want to be asked like, do you need anything to eat all the time." Age 17, Diabetes*
> *"They don't listen, just because it's not very physically visible because I've learnt to hide it, they just don't realise for some reason." Age 16, Chronic Pain*

4. The need to be included in and supported by the school community
    This includes support from peers, staff and the wider school; and inclusion (not exclusion) from activities and events.

> *"I feel like it really clarifies like your disability, doesn't it? It's like 'oh are you going on the trip?' 'No, I can't go' . . . I feel like they are mean quite a lot to me." Age 16, Chronic Pain*

5. The need to build towards their future

This includes thinking ahead to possible careers and grades/subjects they may need in order to access their chosen career pathway. Transitions need to be carefully planned.

> "[To do well in exams and get a good job] have been my goals for so long, I'm not going to stop now because of one thing that happened in my life." Age 17, Oncology

6. The need to develop attitudes and approaches to help them cope in school and have positive mental health

This includes fostering positive attitudes and approaches to cope with the medical condition at school, fostering the positive mental health and emotional well-being of the learner.

> "I think it just made me grow up quite a lot, in a way . . . faster than everyone else, which, I guess, in some ways is good, but in other ways it's just nice to be young and care about less serious things." Age 18, Rheumatology

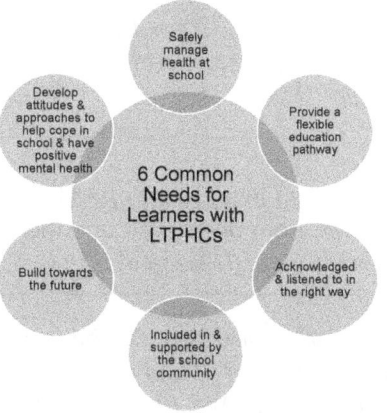

Figure 6.1 Summary of the Six Common Needs of Learners with LTPHCs in school

🔍 Case studies

The following case studies illustrate different approaches learners have experienced at school. These are composite case studies based on INSCHOOL interview data from learners with a range of different medical conditions and their parents, and the experiences seen by the authors.

Billy's story

Billy is 13 and has leukaemia. When diagnosed, he was in hospital for a long time and *'missed almost 2 years of school'*. His mum contacted school to let them know he would not be there for a while. School kept phoning to ask why he wasn't there, which was upsetting.

School remained in contact with the family to check on how he was doing. They sent cards and gifts. Billy's friends kept in touch through social media.

While in hospital and when he felt well enough, Billy had lessons from the hospital education team. The team continued to provide education online once he was discharged but still too poorly to go back to school. They focussed on core subjects.

Billy went back to school initially on a phased return. A multi-disciplinary team meeting including nurses, physiotherapists and school staff drew up an Individual Healthcare Plan outlining his needs. This set out reasonable adjustments like timetabling lessons and providing a lift pass, so he didn't have to climb stairs or walk very far. Billy had a buddy to carry his things. The plan set out what school needed to be aware of to manage his leukaemia, such as not exposing him to chicken pox, and understanding that he may be too tired to concentrate in lessons. School provided him with a tutor in the holidays to help him catch up.

Although an effective plan had been put in place to support Billy, the reasonable adjustments were not always communicated to all staff which led to some setbacks.

'I had lost all my hair because of the chemo, so was wearing a hat in school. Then this teacher just came and whipped it off my head in front of everyone'.

Billy and his mum also felt like school were unaware of the long-term impact of his condition and treatment, which meant they felt less supported as time went on despite his continuing health and education needs.

The school have now made sure that all staff, including supply staff, are aware of the contents of Billy's Individual Healthcare Plan so he feels supported and able to attend school and make progress with his learning.

Mariam's story

Mariam is 16 and has type 1 diabetes and a nut allergy. She doesn't take much time off school except for medical appointments.

When she was younger, she had to wear an armband in the canteen, so staff were aware of her allergy. She didn't like it as it made her 'stand out'. Her secondary school is a nut-free school which has made life easier.

She has an EpiPen in case she has an allergic reaction, but it is kept in the school office and Mariam's mum worries it might not be accessible quickly if she needs it.

Mariam manages her diabetes using a smartphone. She gets into trouble for using it in class because the school has a 'no phones' policy. The other learners make fun of her. They ask her if she's 'diabetic because she eats too much sugar'.

In her Individual Healthcare Plan, it says that if she's poorly the school will call an ambulance, but a parent will need to come to school to accompany her. Mariam and her mum worry that her mum might not be able to get there in time.

As she's got older, Mariam has become more anxious about her conditions and often doesn't want to go to school. Sometimes she lets her blood sugar drop deliberately so she is sent home.

Mariam asked school if she could have any extra access arrangements for her GCSE exams. School did not know how this applied for learners with diabetes. Her mum is worried about her future and how she will manage at college when she has more independence over her own condition and medication. It is not clear who will be responsible for looking out for her.

School have now provided lessons for Mariam's peers about diabetes and allergies, and Mariam has shown them how the app works on her smartphone. They have revised the IHCP to ensure that if her parent cannot get to school to go with her in the ambulance, then a trusted adult from school will go with her. Mariam has been assigned a teaching assistant that she can go to if she is anxious or needs support.

The local hospital school has worked with the exams officer at school to explain what special arrangements can be put in place for Mariam to support her with her exams, and the school careers advisor is accompanying her and her mum to talk to the SEND support team at the local college to discuss arrangements for her post-16 education.

Jasmine's story

Jasmine is 11 and has had colorectal surgery. She has a toilet pass so she can be easily excused from lessons. She feels it makes her 'stand out' from the other learners. Despite a letter from her doctor, the teachers 'don't always believe' she needs to use the bathroom and don't let her go. The toilet is locked during lesson time, and she must go to the office for a key which makes her worry.

Jasmine misses a lot of school and finds it hard to do extra work in her own time when she's off, which makes her anxious. She gets into trouble when she's late for school because of the effects of her medication and for incomplete homework. Other learners 'are cruel' and taunt her. She gets mental health support in school. She worries her mum will 'get into trouble or fined' if she doesn't go to school. All this makes her feel stressed and angry which worsens her condition and so she doesn't want to go to school.

School arranged a meeting with Jasmine and her mum to discuss the issues and produce an updated IHCP. Jasmine is given her own key to the toilet, so she doesn't have to go to the office, and staff have been reminded about her use of the bathroom and alternative arrangements for homework. The attendance team staff have been advised about the possibility of Jasmine being late and the appropriate coding. Mum has been reassured that she will not be fined. PSHE lessons for Jasmine's year group have been revised to include tolerance for people who are different to themselves and to develop a greater understanding about a range of medical conditions.

What do these case studies tell us about practical, cost-effective strategies that you can use in your school?

- Listen to and plan in advance for the learner and families' needs by creating an Individual Healthcare Plan involving the learner, family, school and health staff, setting out the practices to be adopted to meet the learner's needs in each of these six areas.
- Keep in regular communication with the learner and family. Families tell us having a named contact who can advocate for the learner in school is helpful.
- Provide reasonable adjustments such as lift, toilet and time-out passes.
- Consider how to adjust attendance expectations and attendance reward schemes and agree medication requirements and contingencies for medical emergencies. Sensitive use of these adjustments helps learners feel that they do not stand out.
- Ensure consistent application of the agreed adjustments so all staff are aware of what is needed. Consider what is helpful for the family and not just convenient for your school.
- Develop a consistent and strategic approach to counteract lost education and compensate for the impact of the LTPHC on the learner's education. Provide details of what was covered in lesson/s missed and offer catch up and keep up.
- Understand that the learner's medical condition may affect their ability to learn and to concentrate in the classroom, and not all learners will be able to catch up in their own time or want extra work.
- Consider the use of alternative education provided by your local authority for learners with medical needs. Collaborate closely with any alternative providers to ensure that the learner can keep up with their peers and how you can support them to return to school.
- Keep learners connected with school by providing ways for them to keep in touch with peers and teachers. Allocating a buddy/key teacher whilst they are away can support a successful return to school when they are well enough.
- Consider how you include learners in the school community, including access to all subjects and extra-curricular opportunities.

- Check in with your learners with LTPHC regularly, asking whether the adjustments that are in place are working for them, and if they are experiencing bullying or unkind comments about their condition and appearance and what could be done to tackle this.
- Think ahead and plan for transition points by communicating and preparing for important tests and examinations, utilising access arrangements such as extra time and rest breaks, and ensuring learners have access to independent careers information, advice and guidance.
- Consider the emotional well-being and mental health of learners with LTPHC. Often the health condition does not just affect their physical health but affects their emotional well-being and mental health. Look to develop solutions in the school environment or signposting/referring learners and families to external providers. Often just having these needs identified and acknowledged in a compassionate way by school staff can be an especially important first intervention.
- Manage attendance sensitively by knowing who your learners with LTPHC are so that you are not inadvertently punishing and penalising them for being unavoidably off school because they are sick or have medical appointments. Adjust your policies and practices to maximise their attendance. Some may benefit from a phased return or part-time timetable.

Self-reflection

Look at the table below – what do you do in your school to help learners with LTPHC and does any of your practice come into the 'hinder' column?

What helps . . .?	What hinders . . .?
Having a plan to manage medication, education, etc.	Making them feel they 'stand out'.
Adjusting attendance processes and schemes that accommodate the circumstances of learners with medical conditions.	Making them feel bad for missing school or attendance targets.

(Continued)

51

(Continued)

What helps . . .?	What hinders . . .?
Letting learners with diabetes use their smartphone to manage sugar levels.	Making them feel 'left out' of attendance rewards, PE, school trips.
Having a supportive teacher or member of staff to advocate for them and their needs.	Not acknowledging their needs and views on how to manage their condition.
Help for schoolwork missed.	Feeling like they need to come to school when they are poorly, or their parents will be punished.
Being empathetic and understanding.	Not believing what they are telling you.
Having a named contact for parents to approach.	Hassling them when they have a known condition.
Providing details of what has been covered in a lesson.	Locking toilets for learners who need prompt access.
Thinking about future needs – transition, exams.	Not all staff being aware of and using reasonable adjustment.

5 top tips

1. Talk and listen to learners with long-term physical health conditions and their families so you know what their needs are and how you can help to address them. Routinely check in with them to assess and review the effectiveness of the adjustments you have put in place.
2. Know who your long-term physical health condition learner population is because if you know who they are, and how many learners are affected in your school you can better monitor their attendance and plan for their needs both individually and as a cohort.
3. Have a policy for addressing the common school needs of the LTPHC cohort as well as their individual health requirements which include processes to ensure consistent practices are applied

across the whole school. This is particularly important at secondary school when learners are exposed to more teachers.
4. Tackle attendance of this learner cohort by addressing all six needs holistically – medical, education, understanding, inclusion, future, coping and mental health.
5. Have a whole-school strategic approach for these learners to catch up on missed education and to be included equally in school.

References

Hopwood, V., Pini, S., Spencer, B.K.C., & Kitchen, C. (2024). *Qualitative study examining attendance for secondary school learners with long-term physical health conditions.* Continuity in Education, 5(1), pp. 76–89. https://doi.org/10.5334/cie.111

Spencer, B.K., Hugh-Jones, S., Cottrell, D., & Pini, S. (2023a). *The INSCHOOL project: Young people with long-term physical health conditions: An in-depth qualitative study of their needs at school.* Journal of Adolescence https://doi.org/10.1002/jad.12278

Spencer, B.K., Hugh-Jones, S., Cottrell, D., & Pini, S. (2023b). *The INSCHOOL project: Showcasing participatory qualitative methods derived from patient and public involvement and engagement (PPIE) work with young people with long-term health conditions.* Research Involvement and Engagement, 9(1), pp. 1–16. https://doi.org/10.1186/s40900-023-00496-5

7

The psychological impact of attending school with a medical condition

Helen Griffiths

Introduction

Mental health difficulties in learners are increasing, and it is widely published that in the UK almost one in five learners have a diagnosable mental health condition (NHS England, 2023). This does not include learners who have mental health needs that do not fit, or do not quite meet, diagnostic thresholds but nevertheless have an impact on their well-being. What is less well-publicised is that certain groups of learners are more likely to have mental health needs than others – one group of such learners are children with medical conditions. This chapter will explore the relationship between having a medical condition, the psychological impact of this and the impact on education and schooling. Through practical strategies and tips for those working in education, based on feedback from learners and their families, evidence and clinical practice, we hope to give inspiration to people working in education who aim to do their best to support the learners in often challenging and resource-limited circumstances.

Learning from learners, their families and the professionals who support them is at the heart of this chapter and sets the tone; further recommended reading can be found in the references. Thanks go to the many amazing children, young people and families who have informed the thinking behind this chapter, and the professionals who are so dedicated in supporting them.

DOI: 10.4324/9781003478942-9

Medical conditions and mental health

The links between having a medical condition and mental health are numerous and reciprocal. The term 'medical condition' may also refer to a mental health condition, and the Department for Education explicitly includes having a mental health condition in its guidance on supporting children with medical conditions in schools. The points below can relate to any type of medical condition – physical or mental health.

It should be noted that the experience of every learner and their family is different, and one of the most helpful things we can do as professionals is to seek to hear and understand the unique experiences of the family in front of us, and that our job is to help and support. We know that illness parameters alone do not predict psychological outcomes, adjustment or coping; for example, what could be viewed subjectively as a less 'serious' medical condition might lead to a learner and their family really struggling to adapt to the condition, whilst a medical condition that might be objectively more challenging might be met with remarkable coping skills and minimal psychological impact. As professionals, our job is to get to know the whole impact of the condition and how best to support the family.

Below are just some examples of the ways in which having a medical condition can have a psychological impact on the learners and their family and a consideration of possible impacts on education.

Journey to diagnosis

A family's journey to their child's diagnosis can be difficult and may have had a psychological impact. There may have been experiences of not being believed, of struggling to be heard, of many appointments, opinions, tests; it might have been sudden and with no preparation. It's possible that the family will have experienced separations, having to get their child to do something unpleasant or that they didn't want to do, or having to confront a worry that your child may be seriously ill or may die (whether or not those worries were borne out to be true). The journey to diagnosis and the diagnosis itself can bring about a range of feelings – shock, relief, sadness, grief, worry – along with the enormous range of practical aspects of the condition itself.

Understanding the journey to diagnosis can be important in understanding how things are for the learner and their family at school. Common worries are:

- erosion in trust in professionals
- that they will not be believed again
- extra anxiety about separating
- another adult caring for their child
- about how other learners will behave towards their child, who may be perceived as different.

Finding out how the diagnosis came about in a curious, empathic way will provide valuable information to help understand feelings and behaviours that the learners and their family might bring to the education setting.

The demands of the condition itself: procedures, investigations, appointments, medicines . . .

The learners and their family may have gone through an entire range of investigations and procedures, some of which may have been painful, distressing, involve risk and certainly would have been anxiety provoking. The disruption to the learners and their family in terms of appointments and admissions to hospital, both planned and unplanned, will have a further added burden to the family. Treatment regimens including medication, physiotherapy and surgery may be something that the family needs to adjust to longer term. Whilst many conditions are treatable, the feeling of your child being unwell or the possibility of treatment not going smoothly can be overwhelming. The prospect of life never being the same again, or having to develop a 'new normal', integrating the practical demands of the medical condition into everyday life can be a challenge. For the family, there will be practical, logistical, financial impacts which can increase overall stress levels.

There may be a direct link between the procedures linked to the condition and mental well-being. Some learners will develop anxiety in relation to the medical condition or procedures – this may generalise to other settings and situations. There may be increased worry, hypervigilance or wariness about new situations, changes or unfamiliar people. This might mean certain topics or lessons might provoke unexpected anxiety.

Physical impact

Many medical conditions bring with them a physical impact. This could be pain, fatigue, weight loss, weight gain, aches and concentration issues. We know that all these things impact on the school day – how good a nights' sleep you had the night before, how rested you feel when you wake up, how your body feels throughout the day. There can be a vicious cycle whereby you are less able to focus and concentrate because of your body being fatigued or in pain, which means you are less likely to take in information, have the energy to socialise and have a lower threshold for frustration and managing stress. The impact of this can be reduced learning, reduced social opportunities and increased expressed challenging behaviours.

Sense of self-esteem and mood

Having a medical condition can have a direct and indirect impact on the way a learner feels about themselves. Often, the demands of the condition or the condition itself lends itself to a sense of 'difference' – this might mean having to take time off school, visible signs of the condition, having to have extra support or needing to take medication during the day. These seen and felt differences can lead to a sense of questioning, 'Why me?' and sometimes negative thoughts can develop about themself such as 'Everyone thinks I am weird', which can lead to feelings of exclusion. All these things impact on our sense of self and can lead to low mood or depression.

Developmental milestones

Learners typically work through a series of developmental (including social, emotional, cognitive and psychological) milestones. Certain stages are associated with different developmental learning and tasks; this might include learning that the world is safe and predictable, learning to make mistakes, learning who you are as a person. Attachment style can also be impacted, particularly if separations have occurred in early life. Having a medical condition and the extra challenges and demands that this brings, can cause great interference with these tasks at 'typical' times. This is both for the learners themselves and the parent who may also have experienced interruptions to behaviours they might have otherwise engaged in, to support their child to achieve the task. This might look like compensating (e.g. giving more screen time or treats), being more protective (e.g. having to put restrictions on developing independence, difficulty separating) or reassurance seeking (e.g. have school staff done what they have said they would?). For the learners, they might need more scaffolding than other children to achieve developmental milestones as social and emotional opportunities for development might have been missed.

The positives

Having a medical condition is hard for both learners and their family. It is likely that learners will struggle and find things difficult at times. However, we know too that it can lead to many positives for them such as: greater empathy and compassion for others, kindness and caring behaviour, deeper sense of awareness of diversity and its benefits, self-resilience and problem-solving behaviour and many other positive qualities. In the school environment, having a learner with a medical condition can and should be an enriching experience for other learners and professionals. It is a source of inspiration and amazement that learners and their families can manage the challenges they face so well.

The overall impact

For all of us, our experiences in life shape how we think about ourselves, those around us and the world. If we have been scared, afraid or not believed then we are likely to have thoughts and worries about new situations which reflect this. We are also likely to behave in ways that either helped us in those cases, or ways that try to protect us from future situations. These can be *cognitive* and *behavioural* impacts of our experiences. In the education setting, these cognitive and behavioural impacts might show themselves in several ways, through internalising and externalising mechanisms. Understanding the thoughts and behaviour in the context through which they developed is important in putting strategies in place to support the learners and their family.

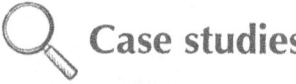 # Case studies

Ayesha's story

Ayesha is a 13-year-old girl with a condition that means she needs to be careful about any injury. Her parents are worried about her doing P.E., and she sits in the classroom and does her homework during the sessions. She sees her friends enjoying themselves, laughing together, pairing up. Her teachers are concerned about her missing out but also are worried about the very real risks if she were to get hurt. Ayesha is visibly upset and has expressed that she feels she is missing out.

Ayesha's teachers spent time with Ayesha discussing how she feels about her medical condition and how it impacts on her in school. They discussed with parents reviewing the Individual Healthcare Plan along with the Clinical Nurse Specialist joining by video call. This helped them better understand the risks involved with P.E. and how these could be safely managed at a level Ayesha's parents and the school were comfortable with; this involved Ayesha practicing shooting netball and becoming 'expert' at this, in pairs with her friends, instead of being involved in the netball game itself.

Self-reflection

- What are the possible psychological impacts of this situation for Ayesha?
- What thoughts might be going through her head?

- What behaviours might you notice?
- What actions and/or solutions could you think of?

Seren's story

Seren is a 6-year-old girl who experienced serious health concerns as a baby, spending 6 months in hospital and then several years going through major surgery and recovery. She presents as a healthy, happy child in school, and although she can be 'clingy' at times, she is easily distracted onto new things. Her parents worry about leaving her in school when she is upset; they frequently contact school to arrange meetings to discuss issues that school consider to be 'minor' and affect all children, and they feel that school do not understand the ongoing health concerns because she 'looks' healthy. When school ask questions about Seren's needs, they feel like Seren's parents get defensive.

The headteacher and class teacher invited Seren's parents to meet to get a better understanding about what things have been like for them and Seren. They learned about how scary Seren's early life was and the very real risk to her. They gained a better understanding of how difficult it is for Seren's parents to see her upset and how they try and prevent her from being sad and from anything 'bad' happening and want to address concerns early. They talked about how they worry that because Seren looks healthy, she will be treated the same as everyone else, when she needs extra care because of her condition. The school team empathised with the parents as to how difficult it must be putting their trust in other adults and agreed on a communication plan and a gentle, graded approach to Seren doing more things independently.

Self-reflection

- What are the possible psychological impacts of the medical condition on Seren's parents?
- What thoughts might Seren's parents be having?

- What behaviour might you see in school?
- How might this be impacting on the relationship with school and education?

Practical, cost-effective strategies that can be used in schools

Many of the most effective strategies that can be used in schools do not cost anything as they involve compassion, thoughtfulness, consideration of language, inclusive practice and putting the learner and their family at the heart of the planning and support. Feeling listened to and understood can be a powerful intervention and will give you ideas generated by the learners and their family that you can put in place.

5 top tips

1. Listen, hear and understand as every learner and their family is different. Their experience will have been different, the internal and external resources they have to manage the medical condition and its impact is different.
2. Think psychological, not 'just' medical: the practical aspects of managing a medical condition can understandably become the focus in school. Questions such as 'What medicine is needed and when and how will we store it?' are important questions to ask, but it is equally important to really understand the emotional and psychological impact of the medical condition for that learner, keeping your questions open and curious. Ensure that emotional, psychological and social aspects are covered in the IHCP.
3. Understand a learner's behaviour and what might lie beneath that behaviour. Refer to top tip 1!

4. Developmental milestones are important – but tread gently: having compassionate, gentle conversations with learners and parents, seeking advice and support from medical teams where needed and coming back to the shared goal of supporting the learners to achieve their potential will help smooth out tension that can arise through worry.

5. Illness does not define identity: ensuring that conversations and interactions focus on other aspects of the child's identity and not the illness at the centre is important. Be mindful of language and positioning, make sure the learner is not labelled in accordance with their medical condition within the school environment and avoid singling out where possible.

References

Bryon, M. & Titman, P. (2019). *Helping your child with a physical health condition. A self help guide for parents*. Hachette, UK.

NHS England (2023). *Mental health of children and young people in England, 2023 – wave 4 follow up to 2017*. Accessed at https://digital.nhs.uk/data-and-information/publications/statistical/mental-health-of-children-and-young-people-in-england/2023-wave-4-follow-up# 10.10.24.

The British Psychological Society (2020). *Talking to children about illness*. Accessed at https://cms.bps.org.uk/sites/default/files/2022-06/Talking%20to%20children%20about%20illness.pdf 10.10.24.

8 The wider curriculum for learners with medical needs

James Gibson

Introduction

When I was first asked to write a chapter for this book, my initial emotion was one of excitement. The opportunity to discuss how to develop a wider curriculum with the intent of supporting learners with medical needs is one that appealed to me. However, this initial emotion was soon replaced by one of panic, as I do not really consider myself an expert in this area, rather a person with lots of experience in working with learners who have medical needs. I would not dream of telling someone whether the wider curriculum that they are implementing is correct or not because one thing we all know is that context is key.

I am therefore using this precious opportunity to highlight what I believe 'the wider curriculum' is, why it is important, and how I have implemented it across my school. I will also attempt to show how it can be assessed and how it benefits those that are receiving it. I intend to do this by taking you through the journey that we have had, starting from the initial identification of an issue, all the way through to where we are now and the impacts we are seeing.

The context of Becton School

As stated above, context is key. I will therefore start with a brief introduction of Becton School and the cohorts that it serves. Our hospital school is one

DOI: 10.4324/9781003478942-10

that teaches across three sites each with a distinctive cohort of learners. We work within a large children's hospital that has six wards and several other smaller units. The learners here have acute medical needs including cancer, acquired brain injury, cystic fibrosis, heart and lung conditions, and many more. We also work in a Tier four CAMHS unit where most learners are in-patients with chronic and complex mental health issues, including depression, eating disorders, psychosis, and suicidal ideation. Lastly, we have a Medical Alternative Provision that we are commissioned to deliver on behalf of our Local Authority that supports learners that are too ill to attend school. The school is part of the Nexus Multi-Academy Trust. The learners here, in the main, have mental health issues linked around anxiety. The learners across all three provisions are all dual registered with their home school while they are with us, and our roll varies between 120 and 170 learners at any one time.

Now that the context is set, we can consider the idea of a 'wider' curriculum. However, before we dive into this, it is worth investigating what a curriculum is and how is it defined. Ofsted define the curriculum as '. . . the substance of what is taught. It is the specific plan of what learners need to know and should be able to do' (Ofsted, 2019). The part of this definition that interests me most is '. . . what learners **need** know and **should** be able to do,. This brings us around to the big question of what should our curriculum look like and why?

Now, for most schools this will be about giving learners the skills, knowledge, and qualifications that prepare them for their future. I am also sure that we can all agree at this point that there are some things we would all say are fundamentals, such as the ability to read, write, talk, and have a functional use of mathematics. In addition to these, we also want a broad curriculum that offers learners the ability to shine in art, sport, the humanities, science, etc.

From my experience, I would argue that the above is sufficient for many learners around the country. However, for learners with additional medical needs, we must consider what is it that they need to know and should be able to do, so that they can go on to have a successful and fulfilling life, that may be above and beyond the normal curriculum due to their individual circumstances. It was this consideration that started our journey into a wider curriculum and caused us to look at what is needed in order to provide what is required for each learner with medical needs.

Assessment of need

Once we had concluded that we needed to offer our learners something more, the obvious question that springs to mind is 'of what'? We started by looking at our varying cohorts and how their experience of life (including school) may differ from the norm, how this might affect them, and what they needed to negate the impact of their medical need.

A common theme for most of our learners was that they had missed disproportionate amounts of education compared to their peers, so they often had anxiety linked to this or it is their anxiety that has caused this. Many also had traumatic experiences either linked to their medical need or caused directly by it.

How these issues manifested themselves was remarkably diverse in different individuals. This led us to develop our holistic progress tracker to assess and monitor a variety of issues that may be affected by the learner's medical need (see online resources).

We decided to assess and monitor a wide range of indicators to get an idea of how their medical needs may be manifesting in the learner's presentation. The scale ranges from 1–6 for the categories with a score of 1 indicating that the learner is currently severely inhibited in this area to the point it is affecting their daily life, and a score of 6 indicating that the learner excels in the area and that it is a strength of theirs. This is completed by staff who have worked closely with the learner after about 6 weeks. Yet this information only gives us part of the picture that we need, as some learners will present very differently at home than they do in school, so we also ask both parents and learners to complete a questionnaire that gives their perspective on the issues at hand. This allows us to get a more rounded view of the learner's current presentation and challenges.

Self-reflection

- Do you undertake any holistic assessments for learners in your school?
- If not, is this something you might consider in the future?

Gathering this information was the easy task. The challenging task that followed was developing a 'wider curriculum' that gives the learners the skills and knowledge they need to succeed given their medical needs. Despite our searching, we could not find an appropriate 'off-the-shelf' resource that we felt would be suitable to our learners needs, so we decided to build our own.

To accomplish this, we collaborated with several outside partners to support us in developing the interventions based on the data that we had. We worked with speech and language therapists, occupational therapists, educational psychologists, art therapists, and CAMHS staff who, alongside us, helped to design interventions to support the learners.

Traditionally, most school interventions are delivered one-to-one by a trained teaching assistant or specialist teacher. However, during the design process, two reoccurring themes came up with the professionals that caused us to rethink this model. The first was that it would be important to support the learner's strengths to improve their self-confidence as well as working on areas where the learner needed additional support. The second theme was how important it was to ensure that the interventions happened both regularly and for a specific amount of time.

If we were going to stick with the traditional model of interventions while also addressing the common themes raised by our various therapists, it became clear that the logistical problem of facilitating 200 interventions a week would be a challenge. These would require staffing, several rooms to be available, and a method of quality assuring the various interventions. When you add this to the operational difficulties of which lessons you withdraw the learners from, and issues of staff absence, it soon became clear that we would need to rebuild our entire timetable so the 'wider curriculum' intervention would be a distinct lesson. This allows timetabling for the delivery of the wide range of interventions at the same time so that no lessons are missed and appropriate staffing can be put in place.

We had 24 different intervention lessons each week, with a half-termly rotation, which gave us the breadth to meet the needs of all learners and support developing their strengths.

The interventions we developed can be categorised in five main areas:

1. Mental health support and resilience
2. Social situations

3. Physical activity
4. Creative exploration
5. Life skills and transition.

Self-reflection

- Can you think of any other areas of interventions that you already use in your school?
- Do you deliver your interventions to individual learners or groups?
- What are your main barriers/enablers to delivering interventions?

Mental health support and resilience

Most of the learners we work with have experienced or are dealing with trauma of one type or another. Being hospitalised with a physical illness can be traumatic depending on the nature of their illness, the life-changing effects their illness may have, and the effects it has on their day-to-day life. This whole experience impacts their emotional and psychological well-being.

It is essential to note that, like you, we are not medically trained so cannot provide therapy. However, by using 'therapeutic interventions', we can support the learners appropriately while they are waiting for the therapy they require and start to support their recovery. Close multiagency collaboration, e.g. with psychologists, social workers, and other professionals, helps us to address the unique needs of each learner.

For example, our resilience intervention is a group intervention that focusses on working through learners' previous issues and challenges and acknowledging the ways they have made progress. By focussing on previous successes, this builds self-confidence for learners to recall and replicate the same approaches.

Social situations

Learners who are admitted to hospital can become very socially isolated. They may lose contact with peers, making them anxious about missing vital interactions and experiences that their wider friendship groups are having. For this cohort, the 'wider curriculum' intervention developed opportunities for learners to connect with their peers, both within the hospital setting and through virtual platforms.

Other learners who struggle with social situations can become situationally mute. This anxiety presents real-life difficulties and obstacles, which if unaddressed will impact on their life chances. We have therefore created an environment that maximises anxiety reduction to allow learners to experience successful interactions with peers, helping them to regain their skills and confidence in this area. An example of an intervention here is our 'chill and chat' sessions. Learners in these sessions gain confidence in conversation skills that are appropriate for the peer group. This graded exposure type programme helps reduce social anxiety and supports all these learners with moving forward.

Physical activity and recreation

Whilst in hospital, maintaining physical activity and recreation opportunities is essential for promoting the physical health, mobility, and well-being of learners. Through collaboration with physical therapists and occupational therapists, we have developed tailored exercise routines and movement activities that accommodate the restrictions linked to the learner's medical needs and supports their recovery. For some learners, the focus needs to be on alternative recreation and physical exercise, but we ensure we include this cohort in group activities as much as possible. The links between physical activity and improved mental health are well documented and thus, where possible, we make this area a priority.

Creative exploration

Creative activities can be therapeutic for all learners, providing a means of self-expression, relaxation, and emotional release; this may be more important than ever due to their medical needs. It is important to offer a range of creative activities and experiences including art, music, drama, pottery, or creative writing, and ensuring that there is a means to facilitate it.

This exploration of creative activities provides a great environment for experimentation with limited risk of failure so offering a boost to learner's morale and self-esteem when they are feeling vulnerable. Participating in a group is also therapeutic in nature.

The 'Creative Corner' intervention introduces new techniques, giving learners the opportunities of low-risk activities that have a creative piece as an outcome.

Life skills and transition

Our life skills and transition interventions are the most personalised interventions that we offer. This is because the nature of the intervention will be dependent on the learner's age, their medical needs, the length of hospital stay, and their next appropriate step. For all learners in KS4 onwards, there is a focus on life skills such as cooking, self-care, money management, health and wellness, and independent travel.

Part of this process is about identifying and supporting a learner's transition to the next placement, taking account of their medical condition. This is done in collaboration with the learners themselves, parents, home school educators, and healthcare providers. As a result, a clear transition plan is established with all stakeholders understanding their role in making the future placement a success.

The impact of the 'wider curriculum'

In all honesty it is hard to know exactly what the impact of the wider curriculum has been, due to the nature of inpatient admission and discharge, meaning that there is significant turnover of our learners. Can we also claim that holistic progress made has been purely down to the interventions that have been delivered? Collecting meaningful data in this area is also a challenge.

However, using our in-house tracker to monitor progress, we do know that most learners make improvements across the domains, and qualitative feedback from staff and learners themselves is that they have made significant progress. We also know that attendance at sessions has improved since the interventions implementation which in turn will improve academic achievement.

We still think that there are improvements we could make, e.g. we are altering the length of the interventions after feedback from staff and learners. We are also looking to develop our current interventions to make them more impactful and are developing new interventions with the wider network of specialists that we work with.

Self-reflection

- Are there any of these interventions that you could replicate simply in your school?
- Could you put in a 'chill and chat' session for your learners with medical needs, just to touch base with them?
- Could you offer creative arts sessions for them as an extra-curricular activity?
- Could these innovative ideas help improve the attendance of these learners?

5 top tips

1. Look at your curriculum more broadly to consider that learner's needs in addition to academic subjects. Involve as many people as possible.
2. Think about how to develop a way of baselining and tracking the holistic progress of learners. Making it simple for staff, learners, and parents to complete is key for making it a success.
3. Undertake an audit of what your staff do and do not know regarding holistic interventions and get outside expertise to help with any training and support. The mix of a 'new pair of eyes' alongside

those who really know the learners makes for an intervention that best suits their needs.

4. Consider putting the interventions on the timetable as a bespoke lesson or there is a risk that they will be cancelled when there are staff absences. It also gives them the recognition they deserve in the curriculum.

5. Do not be afraid to pull interventions that do not work and try something new. The needs of learners with medical conditions can change rapidly so you may need to revise your offer.

Reference

Ofsted (2019). *Education inspection framework 2019: Inspecting the substance of education.* Accessed at https://www.gov.uk/government/consultations/education-inspection-framework-2019-inspecting-the-substance-of-education on 28.10.24.

The use of telepresence solutions

Cath Kitchen and Penny White

Introduction

Telepresence robots are a relatively new innovation in the UK, and their efficacy was part of a research project funded by the Department for Education (DfE) in 2018. This technology is quite distinct from remote learning which, although embraced during the pandemic, currently has become less and less useful for learners with medical needs. Learners with medical needs really benefit from interactions with their peers which lifts their mental health and helps maintain those key relationships which are so important when the learner is ready to transition back into their school. Whilst remote learning can be used to supplement the use of AV1, e.g. through the sharing of resources, collaboration with peers in a remote platform, more and more local authorities and schools are investing in a lending library of these robots to help meet the needs of the increasing number of learners who cannot access school full time due to the impact of their medical conditions.

There are various robots being used in schools at present, but this chapter will focus on the use of the AV1 robot.

The AV1 robot

The AV1 robot was created by the Norwegian company No Isolation and is designed to enable learners who are hospitalised or unwell at home to remain connected to their home school and class. The learner operates

DOI: 10.4324/9781003478942-11

AV1 via a tablet, iPad, or computer, and the learner cannot be seen by their peers. The robot can sit in the learner's seat/on their table/desk in their class, and the learner can interact and communicate with their peers and teaching staff through a microphone and speaker in the body of the robot. Unlike other robots, there is a one-way video stream which is end-to-end encrypted, thus allowing the learner to participate in their class without being seen; this then respects the privacy of the learner who may not wish to be seen due to the impact of their health difficulties. The AV1 also has a series of lights which make up facial expressions to indicate how the learner may be feeling, a series of lights in the 'head' of the robot to indicate if the learner wants to ask a question or just needs to listen and can be rotated round to see others. Only one learner can use the AV1 from a single device at a time.

Outcomes from the DfE research project (2021) and subsequent studies by Fletcher, Bond, and Qualter (2023) outlined the potential benefits of the use of AV1, alongside some of the challenges for its future adoption. All these findings have been supported by our own experience of collaborating with schools who are using AV1.

Benefits of use

- Learners using AV1 show improvement in their attendance, both in the classroom and in social situations such as engaging with peers during breaks. This not only supports the school, but also the learner in seeing their attendance rise and taking away the anxiety of what they might be missing in school and what is happening in their friendship groups.
- AV1 supports learners with their attainment, to at least be able to keep up with their peers despite their illness, as they can access and participate in live lessons alongside their peers.
- Teachers do not have to prepare additional work, nor run any additional lessons. They can also provide feedback in real time so any misconceptions can be addressed.
- The learner shows improved self-esteem and self-confidence as they are enabled to contribute to the class and interact with their peers, all

from the safety of their own home or hospital. This gives them a sense of control over their situation which is particularly important for learners with physical health needs, like cancer, who have so little control over treatment regimes and hospital inpatient admissions.

- AV1 enables the learner to feel that they continue to 'belong' to their home school community. The learner using AV1 is in lessons day-to-day, is aware of events going on in the school, and can maintain social contacts and friends within the school. This also supports an easier transition back to school following the period of absence.
- Teaching staff report that having the learner in their lessons and being able to talk to them, felt that they were really including them in their lessons and the life of the school. They could see the positive impact it had on the learner in terms of their well-being and engagement.
- Parents are positive about their child using AV1 as they can see the benefits of them being able to engage in their lessons and maintain their friendships. They also underlined how much easier it was to get their child back into school after a period of absence, noting a decrease in their anxiety about being away from school.
- No Isolation provide great technological support and advice ensuring that all parties have everything they need to make the use of AV1 successful.

Potential challenges of use

- The cost of AV1 can be prohibitive for some schools and the decision to use it may be impacted by financial restraints. They can be bought outright or hired (current costings can be found on the No Isolation website), and if you own the AV1, there is still a monthly charge to pay for support for any technology queries, replacement, and funding of the 4G access. For learners with certain health conditions, charities may provide funding for the purchase of AV1 or be able to lend one to you. Many local authorities are now also investing in a 'lending library' of AV1s to support their strategy in reducing long-term absence and promoting inclusion in their schools, so reducing their spend on alternative provision. It is worth asking the question!

- Wi-Fi dependency is an important consideration, both in school and in the learner's home. AV1 robots have a 4G card which means it can be used outside the school and on school trips, but in school it needs to be connected to the school system. The IT technician is your best friend in this case. If the Wi-Fi signal is poor in the learner's home, that can be more challenging to address; a stable internet connection is key for the successful operation of AV1.
- Preparation and information sharing, and concerns about security and data protection, are key considerations to AV1 being positively received by staff. It is important that the AV1 is introduced properly, and staff and learners have opportunities to ask questions about how it works, including how data will be protected. Letters need to be sent home to the other learners in any classes so that their parents are aware of the purpose and use of AV1 and have an opportunity to raise questions and concerns. AV1 has a very robust data security and encryption system in place, but it is important that all parties understand and are aware of this.
- Use of AV1 can also increase staff workload, for example preparing worksheets to be sent home or to be emailed to the learner, upload-ing resources to a Google Classroom, and collecting and marking books. Additional workload can also be created in the co-ordination and preparation for use of AV1 in school. This needs to be carefully managed.
- It is important to be aware that the use of AV1 may not always have consistent benefits. For example, the learner engaging with peers may hear all the things they have been doing, making them more aware of what they are missing due to their illness. Older learners sometimes do not like the attention using AV1 brings to themselves and therefore do not like using it.
- Challenges of moving the AV1 robot around to different classrooms in a secondary school requires additional management arrangements. Some schools have the learner's timetable laminated and put round the neck of the robot; others have either a teaching assistant or a peer who is responsible for moving the AV1 around the school. This is less of an issue in primary schools, where classes tend to remain in one classroom.

Self-reflection

- Reading the benefits and challenges of using AV1 above, do you think your school would be willing to use them to support learners with medical needs?
- What do you think may be some of the challenges you might face in your school if you were to use AV1, and how could they be overcome?

⌕ Case studies

Anne's story

Anne is in Year 10 and has a diagnosis of Functional Neurological Disorder/ Conversion Disorder alongside an undiagnosed comorbid presentation of Tourette's type symptoms with tics, and a presenting alter ego following each episode of FND absence. She was absent from her mainstream school for most of the previous academic year, and her recorded attendance for Year 9 was 17%.

During an initial home visit to discuss a planned approach to educational provision, Anne experienced 20 episodes of absence over the duration of 30 minutes.

To cater for her presenting needs, it was agreed with Anne, her family, and the school that the most effective support for her would be the use of a robot from her home to her school.

Reintegrating back into education provoked initial feelings of anxiety, which made Anne's symptoms of the disorder worse. However, this was made manageable by the fact that the learning was accessible via AV1 from her home, and she remained fully supervised and supported by the caregiver who was present daily.

Initially, Anne accessed a learning environment within school for a maximum of one hour per day, which quickly increased to two hours and then three. Anne got to know the other learners in the group 'virtually' using the robot and before long was asking to meet them in person and vice versa.

At this stage, an in-person part-time timetable was put in place for Anne so she could attend school in person, whilst still accessing the learning environment using the AV1 at the other times. Within four months, Anne was back in school full time.

Anxiety was significantly reduced and consequently the frequency of episodes of absence were seen to diminish. These were managed with an IHCP alongside an appropriate risk assessment.

Anne went on to successfully complete Year 11 with GCSEs in English Literature, English Language, Religious Education, Biology, Maths, and functional skills ICT. She has successfully moved on to college.

Joshi's story

Joshi is a Year 12 learner who was undertaking his A levels. He was immunosuppressed and advised to shield at home and not attend school for a three-month period. This would have meant that he would have been unable to complete his A-level courses.

Joshi's home school collaborated with the hospital school so that AV1 was used in all his Alevel lessons, giving him access to a full-time school timetable whilst he completed his three months of shielding. He went on to return to school and successfully complete his A-evel programme of study.

The following statements illustrate the impact for the teacher, and Joshi.

Joshi's teacher:

It was so helpful to be able to hear Joshi so clearly and see the emotions he was expressing. We were even able to use the robot in a paired discussion which made it feel as though he could actively participate in the lesson. Joshi's engagement and progress within lessons was aided using his AV1 robot. The robot allowed me to assess his learning more accurately during the lesson and question him about the content to check for understanding. It also allowed him to engage with class discussion and contribute his ideas which would then receive feedback from me and other learners within the class. The use of AV1 also allowed him to look at ideas which were written on the whiteboard or the presentation, which allowed him to see and take in information to further support his learning. AV1 ensured that Joshi was present within the lesson which I believe also aided his learning as he could hear explanations given by me and other learners and had the ability to ask for guidance surrounding any new concepts or ideas if needed.

Joshi's views:

The introduction and use of AV1 assisted me in slowly getting back to some sense of normality as I had previously been shielding at home for quite a while. By having this robot, I was able to interact with my peers and teachers which made me feel elated and part of the class again. Also, it took the stress off my shoulders by being able to discuss any problems with the teachers when they arose instead of having to email teachers later, and it helped with the self-teaching knowing that I could access support in the classes. I am so grateful for the opportunity to use this technology. It is a wonderful invention and so helpful to me as well as many other learners across the country for accessing education effectively.

Bailey's story

Bailey was in Year 11 and was experiencing the long-term effects of COVID-19 with symptoms of ongoing chronic fatigue and malaise. Attendance for the previous academic year was 40%. Despite the flexibility of a part-time timetable, he was unable to keep up with the physical demands of getting up, getting ready for school, travelling to school, and negotiating the demands of walking to multiple subject areas around a busy large mainstream school environment.

The part-time timetable was maintained, alongside a reduced GCSE subject offer. An AV1 robot was installed in all Bailey's GCSE subject lessons giving full accessibility to the agreed educational provision. Using the AV1 meant that Bailey could have full access to the part-time reduced GCSE offer without the demands of the practical elements stated within the context above.

Essentially, Bailey could access his education from home which allowed him to fully rest when he was not in class. Reducing the physical demands requiring him to be 'present' meant that all his energy could be prioritised for the cognitive demands of the curriculum.

Bailey went on to successfully complete Year 11 with GCSEs in English Literature, English Language, Religious Studies, Biology, and Maths.

Self-reflection

- Have a look at the No Isolation website for more information and case studies, https://www.noisolation.com/uk.

5 top tips

1. Do not be daunted by the cost of buying or hiring an AV1 – check with your LA and charities to access funding.
2. Ensure that you prepare everyone for the implementation of AV1 – staff, governors, parents of other learners in the class, parent of the learner who is unwell, IT technicians, and the learner themselves.
3. Make use of the support from No Isolation, no matter how small your query.
4. Be creative in how you use AV1, and ensure that you include extra-curricular activities, school trips, and social times.
5. Celebrate your inclusive practice and the difference you are making to learners with medical needs!

References

Department for Education (2021). *Learning from practice: Reintegration to mainstream settings from Alternative Provision Innovation Funded projects.* Accessed at https://assets.publishing.service.gov.uk/media/60a 685b0e90e071b5d705c75/DfE_Key_finding_Reintegration.pdf accessed 09.04.24.

Fletcher, M., Bond, C., & Qualter, P. (2023). *Using AV1 robots to support learners with physical and emotional health needs.* Educational Psychology in Practice, 1–18. https://doi.org/10.1080/02667363.2023.22 69082

No Isolation (2024). *Introduction video for AV1 robots* https://www.noisolation. com/uk#av1-video accessed 09.04.24.

Working with your local hospital school/medical Alternative Provision

Janet Doherty, Joanna Beswick, Emma Cunha, and Gwen Rees-Moffitt

Introduction

This chapter will explain how your local hospital school/medical Alternative Provision/Local Authority Home Tuition Services (referred to as medical AP in this chapter) could support you and your staff to identify, assess, and support those learners with medical needs on roll at your school or setting.

Our ideas are closely aligned both to the Tier 1 working model outlined in the SEND and AP Green Paper (DfE, 2023) and to the model for medical AP developed by National Association for Hospital Education (NAHE) members. As local support available for schools varies across the country, the chapter will set out the type of support you should expect to find and to be able to access within your local area.

We know that once a learner has stopped attending school it can be a lengthy process to get them back into full-time education. Our chapter will address these points:

- How to quickly identify and work with a learner who is at risk of becoming a long-term non-attender, and we will offer practical strategies for you to use.

DOI: 10.4324/9781003478942-12

- We will offer our top tips, based on our experience, of how to re-engage your learners if they have become entrenched within their home and are unable to leave.

Throughout the chapter, we will refer to some of our learners who have taught us so much.

How to identify learners in need

Schools play a key role in identifying early indicators for learners who are experiencing difficulties in attending school. For learners with a medical condition, it is vital to understand how the medical condition may impact on their everyday life and what adaptations need to be made within the classroom and in the wider school environment so that the learner can continue to access their education.

Many learners with medical conditions also experience elevated levels of anxiety, and attending school may be challenging for a variety of reasons that may be not just about their illness. Fully understanding what is at the root of these high levels of anxiety is important to be able to plan appropriate support for the individual learner.

If your staff are skilled and trained to look out for early indicators of unmet needs, they can ensure appropriate interventions are quickly put in place for individual learners.

It is essential that there is strong collaboration between the teams across the school.

Self-reflection

- What mechanisms do you have in your school to identify early indicators for leaners who are struggling to come into school?
- Have you identified your learners with medical conditions and looked at their attendance?
- How effective is your communication between school and home?

The key to early identification is to know your learners. Having that knowledge is a powerful starting point, and developing positive, strong relationships with families will enable you to provide the right support which may involve other multi-agency professionals. Effective communication between home and school will also allow you to share any concerns with parents at the earliest opportunity, rather than waiting until the concern escalates and the learner stops attending school altogether.

How to gather learner voice – Do we ask the right questions in the right way?

Invariably, the best way to find out how to support a learner is to ask them. This is a step often missed by busy staff in busy schools. Assumptions are often made about learners and their families, their situation or circumstances, and plans are decided by professionals without careful and thorough consultation with the learner and their families. The key point is to never assume, question everything, and always look beyond the obvious.

If the plan put in place to support a learner to access education is not successful or does not deliver the expected impact, this can leave staff feeling frustrated and learners and their families feeling despondent. You will usually seek to implement plans and approaches which are easiest to deliver as this means that the plan is most likely to be sustainable and cost-effective. However, this approach will only realise the positive outcomes if the plan directly addresses the learner's barriers to education or school attendance. You should not assume to know these barriers; your learners are individuals with distinct personalities, previous experiences and needs, and their barriers to accessing education or attending school can be wide-ranging and varied.

Asking the right question is already half of the solution to the problem: make sure you ask the right question in the right way.

Speaking with the learner needs to be the first intervention. You need to make every effort to hear the voice of the learner; and in hearing, you should listen. It may be that accessing the learner's voice is difficult, but it is unlikely to be impossible, so you may have to be creative in how you capture this voice, acknowledging that it may be challenging, and it may take time.

Investing the time and resources in capturing the voice of the learner is important for several reasons:

- By listening, you are better able to identify the barriers to attendance and are more likely to be effective in addressing those barriers.
- You have a legal, statutory, and moral obligation to listen to the voice of the learner.

The current *SEND Code of Practice: 0–25 years* (DfE, DoH, 2014) places an emphasis upon involving the learner in decision making at both individual and strategic levels. This reinforces the statutory role schools play in capturing the voice of the learner.

The importance of asking the question is indisputable; the method for acquiring the answer is key to the success of this process. The Children's Act (1989) requires local authorities to give due regard to a learner's wishes when determining what services to provide. To this end, local authorities are required to publish their 'Voice of the Child' strategy; this is a good starting point for you as the strategies used by professionals working for the local authority, such as social workers, can be directly transferable to your staff.

Self-reflection

- What current systems and processes do you have in place in your school to enable you to listen to the voices of learners?
- Are they effective and how do you know?

Best practice in listening to the voice of the learner

In the research paper 'Pathways to participation: Openings, opportunities, and obligations' (2001), Harry Shier outlines five levels of participation when taking the views of learners into account: Learners are:

- listened to
- supported in expressing their views

- involved in the decision-making process
- learners' views are considered
- learners share power and responsibility for decision making.

The challenges for you in adopting these approaches may be:

- Accessing the learner may be problematic.
- The learner may be unwell and not leaving their home or spending prolonged periods in their bedroom which provides logistical difficulties. You need to adopt a persistent and solution-focussed approach whereby every effort is made to access the learner in an empathetic, compassionate, and considered manner.
- The learner is struggling to articulate their barriers to attending school or accessing education. You must ensure that your most skilful practitioners are deployed to support the learner to communicate their needs.
- You may be wary of making large-scale adaptations to your school for an individual learner for fear that this may set a precedent and 'open the floodgates' for other learners to expect what could be seen as 'preferential' treatment. Please do not refrain from giving a learner the support they need from fear of the reaction of others.
- Avoid quickly dismissing requests from a learner even though they may seem to be outlandish and impossible. Give them consideration, and explain why they may not be possible, looking for alternative solutions.
- Investment in time and resources may seem like an unnecessary expense and a drain on your already scarce finances, but this approach is much more likely to see a positive impact than a phone call, a text, or an email.

What support can you access from your medical AP/hospital school, and what interventions are possible?

If you feel you have exhausted all your knowledge and expertise, you can begin to feel as if you are not the correct provision for the learner, or you think you may have to consider more punitive approaches such as fines for lack of attendance or exclusions for behaviour. These approaches, whilst understandable, are often damaging and perpetuate a culture of blame, where there is an assumption of a level of control on the learner or parent's part, rather than viewing the behaviour as a communication of need. There is a risk of seeing these external behaviours as a choice, when often, if not always, it is an expression of an unmet need.

This is when your medical AP may be able to offer key advice and support, drawing on the expertise that exists in their own settings and services.

Whilst each medical AP may operate slightly differently, the sorts of services you may find available are:

- Support through advice and guidance phone calls and meetings, where you can outline the learner's needs and receive support.
- Support and signposting to relevant services and documentation.
- Support with access to remote learning.
- Staff training.
- Support for senior leaders.
- Specialist support for specific needs on how to best adapt your school environment for neurodiverse learners and make 'reasonable adjustments' for the learner's needs.

Advice and support from outreach services can often support and challenge schools to reframe their thinking, is cost effective, and can lead to early intervention to prevent escalation of the difficulties which can lead to not attending school.

Emotionally based school non-attendance (EBSNA) is a rising concern across the country. Your local medical AP can provide guidance on how best to support a learner with EBSNA., which may include recognising that EBSNA can be linked to other SEND needs, which may have been missed or mis-diagnosed.

When observed behaviours may be a form of communication

Many staff in medical AP have a level of expertise in trauma-based practice, mental health support, and how to support learners with autism and

ADHD; this helps them to spot where behaviour may be a communication of need, and they can support you with strategies to help the learner manage this need.

 Case studies

Arlo's story

Arlo regularly disrupts and leaves the classroom. The school considered that he may be a learner who is reaching sensory overload and needs a rest break or some sensory input. 'Sensory circuits' are sensory integration and processing interventions which include a sequence of physical activities that are designed to alert, organise, and calm the young person. Since the school put in the support for Arlo to regulate using sensory circuits, often first thing in the morning or after break and lunchtimes, they have seen greater success in preventing dysregulation during the school day. This is a quick intervention, and teaching assistants can deliver these sessions each day; the activities can be adapted to meet the needs of the individual learner.

Sharon's story

Sharon's teachers were reporting that she seemed to be behaving in ways that were 'seeking attention'. The MHS SENCO pointed out that this may be about Sharon 'seeking connections' and that she may need support in managing this need. An example of this connection-seeking behaviour that Sharon exhibited was where she repeatedly picked her skin and then sought medical attention in lessons for small cuts or picked scabs. In this scenario, Sharon called on the attention of an adult who then sent her to a first aider to have the wound treated. In this way, Sharon was receiving the nurture she was seeking, and teachers were asked to consider if she was reaching a point in the lesson where she needed a rest break to regulate. Sharon was offered a sensory circuit (see above) and a designated safe space with an emotionally available adult, and this resource prevented Sharon's subsequent unhealthy connection-seeking behaviours. The school could not always guarantee having an adult available in a designated safe space, so timetabled regular drop-ins for Sharon with this adult to support her, thus meeting her needs.

David's story

David is in Year 3 at primary school and has experienced adverse child-hood events resulting in him wetting regularly in the school day, which was frustrating school staff. The hospital school staff asked school to consider if this could be a connection-seeking behaviour. David wets, then receives 1:1 nurture, care, sympathy, and reassurance from the adult. This reassures him that he is cared for, and his needs will be met. Again, like Sharon scheduling time for David with an emotionally available adult to receive this reassurance in school started to reduce the number of incidents of wetting. The reassurances used in this case were meet and greet in the morning, just before/after lunchtime, and then at the end of the school day before David headed home, to allow him to unpick any events in the day and encourage him to attend the next day.

Learning from our case studies

- Where learners feel supported, the outcome is more likely to be positive.
- Prepare the learner for the communication opportunity if necessary and consider the best conditions for maximising participation.
- Use natural encounters and everyday interactions to elicit views; it does not have to be a 'special event'.
- Give learners the opportunity to share their views without their parents/carers present if they would like to do so.
- Plan ahead – and get the questions right. Why are you asking? What information do you need? How are you going to find out? Who is the best person to have the conversation? What actions are you going to take because of finding out the information?
- Match the tools and methods you use to collect information with the needs of the learner.
- As far as possible, present the true voice of the learner and avoid adapting the language for adult purposes.

- Use your more experienced and senior staff members to visit the homes of hard-to-reach learners or carefully select staff with a positive relationship with the learner to meet with them and their families.
- Creative approaches to gathering the views of the learner are also more likely to see successful outcomes. For example, learners with situational mutism can use card sort activities to organise what is important to them: what makes them happy, what makes them feel confident and comfortable, and what makes them feel unhappy or worried. For this to be effective, a skilled staff member would offer prepopulated cards for the learner to sort, as well as some blank cards for the learner to add concepts and ideas which may emerge as the activity progresses.
- Using the 'What Matters Island' template (NDTi, 2024) can be useful in gathering views of learners who struggle with communication. This simple template is designed to help learners talk and co-produce a summary of what matters to them and what they would like to happen in the future. This visual approach is particularly helpful for neurodiverse young people as there is a clear structure for the dialogue, and facilitators are encouraged to stick to clear timings for each section.
- Successful outcomes are more dependent on attitude and an approach that requires specialist skills and knowledge.
- It is important to balance the views of the learner with the welfare of the learner and effective safeguarding practice.

Practical solutions for other school pressures

- Your school may feel pressured to reinforce high expectations for behaviour and maintain high levels of attendance which make you reluctant to implement alternative arrangements for individual learners, fearing negative reactions across your school community. Medical AP teams can support you and your school to recognise that reasonable adjustments are required to enable the learner to attend school. For example, a strict uniform policy may make you feel you cannot allow an autistic student with sensory needs to wear tracksuit bottoms or leggings, when this reasonable adjustment may mean that the learner attends school. You can manage adaptations by communicating clearly and sensitively with your community about the adjustments made. Schools tell us that it is fear of the reaction of others that prevents them from making changes for individuals.

- Mainstream schools are often concerned about how reduced timetables may be perceived, but these are remarkably effective in reintegrating learners back into their mainstream setting over time or enabling learners with a medical condition to attend. Do not feel deterred from providing the timetable a learner needs. Reduced timetables are legal if they are reviewed every six weeks. They are only illegal when they are in place to prevent access to full-time education. Your medical AP team can support you to create reduced timetables and give you and your staff the confidence and courage to implement them.

Self-reflection

- How good is your school at making 'reasonable adjustments' to support the attendance of learners with medical conditions? Think about the number and types of arrangements you currently have in place.
- Search for 'medical AP, hospital school, home tuition services' in your local area, and reach out and make contact. Check out their website and see what support they can offer you. They want to help!

5 top tips

1. Develop systems for early identification of learners who may be at risk.
2. Capture the voice of the learner.
3. Make adaptations to meet their needs.
4. Seek advice and support from professionals in your area, including medical AP teams.
5. Never give up or lose sight of the young person. Persist.

References

Department for Education, Department of Health (2014). *Special educational needs and disability code of practice: 0 to 25 years.* Accessed at https://assets.publishing.service.gov.uk/media/5a7dcb85ed915d2ac884d995/SEND_Code_of_Practice_January_2015.pdf 26.8.24

Department for Education (2023). *Special Educational Needs and Disabilities (SEND) and Alternative Provision (AP) Improvement Plan. Right Support, Right Place, Right Time.* Accessed at: https://assets.publishing.service.gov.uk/media/63ff39d28fa8f527fb67cb06/SEND_and_alternative_provision_improvement_plan.pdf 26.08.24.

National Development Team for Inclusion (2024). *What Matters Island.* Accessed at https://www.ndti.org.uk/resources/publication/what-matters-island 26.08.24.

Shier, H. (2001). *Pathways to participation: Openings, opportunities, and obligations.* Children & Society, Vol. 15, pp. 105–117. DOI: 10.1002/CHI.617.

UK Government (1989). The Children Act. Accessed at https://www.legislation.gov.uk/ukpga/1989/41/contents 26.08.24.

Hidden in plain sight
Best practice for supporting learners with acquired brain injury (ABI)

Emily Bennett and Gemma Costello

Introduction

The lived experience of learners with acquired brain injury (ABI) in schools underpins this chapter. When considering the rationale, no one is better positioned than the learners themselves to explain why the understanding of ABI within the education system is essential. In their own words, the young people from the National ABI in Learning and Education Syndicate (NABLES), Young Experts by Experience with ABI group (YEBEABI) set the scene to this important topic:

> *When do you tell someone you have an ABI? You get such a different reaction, I'm not any different to the person you were talking to 5-minutes ago, what does it really mean to you? As a group of young people, we have experienced Traumatic Brain Injuries (TBI), Encephalitis, Subdural Empyema, and an arterio-venous malformation (AVM). These have occurred following illnesses, accidents, skating down a hill, and even fainting at the doctors. Our lives shifted two thousand different gears, one day life was ticking along and the next it's a completely different one. Attending school, preparing for GCSEs or A levels and the next thing you know, everyday tasks such as shopping or heading into town feel really overwhelming, or you are setting off airport security alarms with a titanium plate in your head . . . let alone returning to school! We are like a different person on the other side, we return to education with a hidden disability, wanting to feel*

DOI: 10.4324/9781003478942-13

like ourselves, shouting to be heard so others know how to help. But sometimes the smallest step in the right direction ends up being the biggest step of your life. Thank you to the people who take 5 minutes to understand or learn, it changes the game astronomically! It doesn't take long to 'get it', we aren't that hard to understand, please take the time to learn. One thing we are always thankful for is our families, our teachers who took the time to understand . . . and each other, within the group!

Like these young people, most learners with an ABI will return to or start in mainstream schools. Many will experience new needs following their injury or illness and will require support from you to assist in their recovery, adjustment, and progress. Despite this, we understand that you may know little about ABI and may frequently feel unprepared and ill-informed to manage the presenting needs of this group (Linden et al., 2013; Howe and Ball, 2017). This chapter will introduce you to ABI, including the important things to understand about this condition, particularly when experienced during childhood and adolescence. We will explore presenting needs in the classroom alongside interventions and resources that enable participation and promote learning within your school.

What is an ABI?

An ABI is an injury to the brain that is acquired after a period of typical development and is identified as the leading cause of death and disability in childhood (Forsyth and Kirkham, 2012) with over 40,000 learners in the UK experiencing some kind of ABI every year. ABI can be the result of accident/trauma (e.g. falls, road traffic accidents, assaults), infection or illness (meningitis, encephalitis, empyema), stroke, brain tumour, or hypoxic events (e.g. near-drowning, cardiac events) to the brain.

ABIs can range from mild (e.g. concussion) to severe, with the subsequent need for support in school ranging from simple adaptations in the weeks after an injury, to long-term individual support or even changes in school placement. ABI can impact learners across the SEND Code of Practice's four broad areas of need; changes in behaviour and emotions are common, as are cognitive, physical, and sensory difficulties (see Figure 11.1). Many learners also experience high levels of neuro-fatigue and changes in their communication and social skills.

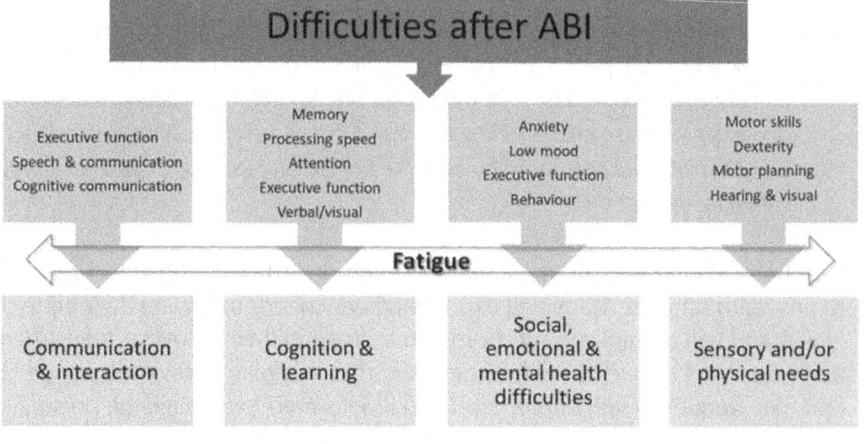

Figure 11.1 The impact of ABI on a child's functioning and the four broad areas of need

The challenges of childhood ABI

There are myths within society that children's brains have an ability to 'bounce back', due to brain plasticity, and that the population of learners with ABI is very small. This perpetuates the lack of pathways and provision for these groups with under-recognition and limited provision for them beyond acute medical settings. Children then return to, or start their school with, rehabilitation needs that are often unrecognised, and with limited awareness of how to support them at what is a crucial time for maximising neuroplasticity and recovery within the brain.

One of the key challenges with childhood ABI is its 'dynamic' and often hidden impact. The effects of the ABI are determined by its nature and severity, as well as the age and developmental stage of the learner at the time of injury/illness. As a result, the true impact of an ABI may only become evident as the learner's brain develops across childhood and adolescence, meaning support within education settings must evolve as the learner's presenting needs emerge.

It is important to consider that, "Childhood ABI does not operate within an equal opportunities' basis . . . whereby adverse socio-political factors such as poverty, financial disadvantage, less enriched social environments, and intergenerational factors (social, psychological and genetic) combine to elevate the risk of acquiring an injury" (Jim et al., 2022). Learners from socio-economically deprived areas, for instance, have an increased risk of sustaining a traumatic brain injury (TBI) (Amram et al., 2015), and pre-existing neuro-developmental vulnerabilities also put learners at increased risk following ABI. Those with a diagnosis of ADHD, for example, have an increased likelihood of engaging in risk-taking behaviours, impulsive actions, and being inattentive within their environment, all of which can further increase the risk of TBI (Cooke et al., 2022). There is also a cumulative risk that follows childhood brain injury that sees increased likelihood of exploitation, academic and vocational underachievement, and contact with criminal justice and mental health services (Williams, 2010; Gracey et al., 2014).

The challenges of providing education after ABI

After an ABI, learners and their families are often faced with adjusting to a 'new normal' in many areas of their lives. Returning to their education setting is frequently described as one of the most difficult aspects, with many finding school both familiar, yet completely different. There are several reasons this transition can be so challenging, including a lack of training about ABI for teaching staff, the time taken for the SEND system to respond to acquired needs (e.g. Education Health and Care Plans process/funding applications), and a scarcity of pathways and planning to ensure there is collaborative support across health and education (Bennett, Thomas, and Woolf, 2022).

Due to the evolving nature of ABIs, ongoing support and adjustments are often needed within the school and classroom throughout a learner's time in education. This can present challenges, and research demonstrates that information about ABIs is often lost over time (Howe and Ball, 2017). This is particularly evident where young people have made a positive physical or medical recovery, or have a visible difference associated with their illness/injury (e.g. spinal cord injury, visual/hearing needs), when ongoing cognitive/emotional/social needs can remain hidden beneath the surface. It can also be a challenge in milder injuries that have a prolonged impact on a learner's participation, or for those who experience an injury in their early years before their time in formal education. Where the ABI is unrecognised or forgotten, there are risks of misattribution and misinterpretation of difficulties and an investment in interventions that may not be successful in the short or longer term (Limond, Adlam, and Cormack, 2014). This highlights the importance of information sharing, particularly at points of transition, when the new demands of the school environment may present additional challenges and expose previously hidden areas of need, e.g. executive function.

Self-reflection

- Do you know if you have any learners in your school who have an ABI?
- Are your processes for sharing information about learners with ABI sufficient, particularly around transitions?
- How can you ensure learners with ABI are continually monitored so any arrangements they may require are in place?

School as a rehabilitation environment

Rehabilitation after ABI is an ongoing process in the context of a developing brain, with numerous windows of opportunity for promoting recovery, re-learning and acquiring skills, and compensating for difficulties. Schools have the potential to offer a positive environment to present new, age-appropriate challenges, support adaptation, and promote the building (and rebuilding) of brains!

McCarron and colleagues' (2019) review of learners' goals following ABI provides an important reminder of how important school is to the learners themselves. Their chosen rehabilitation goals prioritised re-entry to school, understanding from teachers, and participation within education (McCarron et al., 2019). Importantly, when we get support and adaptation within education settings right, we know that outcomes for learners are much improved (e.g. Todis and Glang, 2008), reducing the many potential negative consequences otherwise associated with childhood ABI.

Working with learners with an ABI in schools

Starting education with an ABI

One of the challenges presented to schools is the hidden nature of ABI. Where a learner has acquired their injury at an early age, the school are reliant on information being shared by families or pre-school provision at the time of admission. It is possible that for several reasons, including the positive physical recovery made by many young learners, and the lack of understanding of the longer term and hidden implications of early injury, teachers may find themselves unaware of the needs of these learners in their classroom. Including questions about a history of ABI on school entry forms is an important starting point for identification of early ABIs. When early ABI is identified or reported, enhanced transition arrangements are often beneficial to ensure parents and teachers can openly communicate about any challenges and possible emerging needs in Reception classes and beyond. It is at this point when ABI-related difficulties with language, attention, sensory difficulties, fine-motor skills, and emotional/behavioural regulation can become particularly apparent.

Self-reflection

- Do you currently have any questions on your school entry forms about any history of ABI?

Returning to education after ABI

It is important to adopt a collaborative, team-based approach when a learner is returning to education after an ABI, to ensure their return is thoroughly planned, their needs are communicated to all involved, and appropriate preparations made in advance. This might involve thinking about:

- The need for an Individual Health Care Plan (IHCP, see Chapter 3), and/or Education Health and Care Plan (EHCP)
- Training for staff and peers
- Adaptations to the environment, curriculum, and teaching methods
- Coordination of multi-professional meetings
- Planning of additional provision.

The more thorough the planning, the more likely the learner will be able to make and maintain a successful return to school.

Ensuring a learner feels 'connected' to their class and school during the period of absence is important; cards and video messages from class-mates/peers, using live video links or telepresence robots, and creating a class diary to keep them updated can be helpful and can reduce feelings of isolation from peers and anxiety about returning to school. Once a learner is medically fit and able to cope with school, starting a phased return should be encouraged as soon as possible. Initially this might just be for short periods at a time, with a focus on participation and social support, as well as learning.

The National Acquired Brain Injury in Learning and Education Syndicate (NABLES) provides umbrella guidance for a best practice model, supporting the transition from health to education services (ABI Return, 2021). The group have also published guidance for schools/colleges on supporting a stepped return to education after concussion (NABLES, 2023). Examples of return to education pathways (e.g. The Nottinghamshire ABI (Sam White) Pathway and Guidance) (Hammill et al., 2019) can also offer helpful insight for education, health, and social care professionals, as well as families. In all such guidance, central principles include:

- Planning and preparation
- Communication and training
- Flexibility
- Child/young person at the centre
- Focus on participation and inclusion.

Figure 11.2 ABI return: Best practice principles for supporting return to education after ABI

Transition between schools

The transition between primary and secondary school often presents a significant challenge for a learner who might be going from a highly supported small learning environment to one where there are greater expectations of independence, organisation, and flexibility and executive functioning skills. The learner also relies on their schools and professionals to ensure an effective transfer of information that facilitates a shared understanding of their experience, needs, and what works in their ongoing rehabilitation and education. Enhanced transitions and planning of regular meetings with the learner, parents/carers, and supporting staff is important. Pupil passports can support a learner to share their strengths, experiences, and needs within the new setting, and provision of a Key Worker with a strong understanding of ABI, and the learner's history, can be particularly beneficial.

Whole school approaches

Awareness of ABI in the school system is one of the greatest factors that promotes ongoing rehabilitation. When staff understand ABI and promote interventions consistently, it enables the learner to access the educational setting with understanding and commitment to their ongoing recovery and development.

It is widely recognised that schools have limited access to training on brain development and more specifically ABI. There is a range of freely available information and training for schools, from charities (see Resources section) and NHS professionals, which can support teaching staff in developing a basic level of awareness of paediatric brain development and the potential implications and considerations following injury.

Developing an understanding of ABI creates opportunities for whole school approaches that benefit the learner within school, demonstrating a commitment to their recovery. Considerations might include

- Planned transition meetings between teachers
- Timetabling adjustments

- Flexible course arrangements (e.g. reduced number of subjects at GCSE)
- The creation of spaces that promote rest and recovery
- Clarification when applying pastoral policies that promote an understanding of ABI and the potential emotions, trauma, or behaviours that a learner may present within the school environment
- Where learners wish to share their story, celebrating narratives of resilience in the face of ABI, acknowledging diversity and celebrating learner's stories.

Self-reflection

- What whole school approaches do you currently have in place that might support your learners with ABI?
- Do you know where you can access training for your staff on supporting learners with ABI?

Class-based interventions

Every learning task provides the learner with ABI an opportunity to discover what works for them in the classroom. For those who have had a period of learning/education prior to their injury, they need to understand, explore, and adapt to their new acquired needs. Learning in the classroom has the potential to either promote a positive connection with their pre-injury identity or, where new needs are not recognised or met, it can lead to patterns of avoidance and frustration. It must be a priority to ensure learners have the support required to pace their approach to learning, manage their fatigue, and assist them in discovering their strengths and skills so they can adapt and create a positive sense of themselves as a learner.

Much of what works for these learners is connected to quality-first teaching, and inclusive interventions that promote access to the curriculum for all, including:

- Being aware of potential spiky profiles of strength and needs that are common after ABI, understanding these can ensure learners success and progress
- Providing structure to lessons and tasks, reinforcing steps to break down instructions and tasks
- Reducing cognitive load by removing unnecessary tasks that do not meet with the learning objective, e.g. provide worksheets, reduce copying from the board
- Giving time for completing tasks or reducing the number of items to be completed in a lesson
- Providing rest and movement breaks within and between lessons to support fatigue
- Understanding the learner's needs and that these are likely to change or emerge over time with development.

Further information about what you might notice in the classroom regarding key areas of difficulty after ABI and suggestions for tools and adaptations that may be useful are detailed in Table 11.1.

When working with learners with ABI, there are also a number of further considerations it can be helpful to bear in mind which are detailed below.

Broad and evolving needs

Targeted interventions also need to consider a learner's needs across physical, sensory, attention, organisation, planning, self-monitoring, emotional regulation, processing, language, communication, and fatigue. These approaches will likely need to change over time in response to development, e.g. a younger learner with executive functioning needs will have these well understood in the context of early development with appropriate scaffolds in place. Over time however, as the support and scaffolds of the learning environment are removed, with expectations for young people to gain independence in their learning, the emerging needs may become evident, and a more targeted approach may be required.

Neuro-fatigue

Neuro-fatigue is often a significant issue after an ABI, and one many educators feel unfamiliar with. Teachers will need to support learners in pacing their activities and in taking rest breaks before they reach the point where they are too fatigued to learn or engage any further. It may be necessary for you to consider whether the timetable or the number of subjects a learner is studying can be adjusted to allow for planned gaps in learning and adequate opportunities for rest. A monitoring system, such as a rating scale or the child's 'battery level', can be beneficial for use by the learner themselves and those supporting them. Ideally, we want to teach learners to be able to self-monitor and manage their fatigue independently, but this is likely to require scaffolding from staff, with frequent review before they can do so successfully.

Important points to consider when dealing with learner's neuro-fatigue:

- Be proactive rather than reactive to fatigue
- Encourage/facilitate regular 'brain breaks' where cognitive demands are reduced as much as possible
- Recognise key contributors to fatigue and try not to have too many at one time – intersperse 'red/brain drain' activities with 'green' restorative activities
- Support learners to prioritise and pace
- Remember participation is not just learning!

The cumulative impact of ABI

While many learners will benefit from quality first teaching and adaptations, it can be necessary to explore additional bespoke support that may be required for some. Furthermore, for many learners, while specific needs can be supported successfully using well-recognised strategies, it is the interaction between different needs and the combined effect of fatigue which can prove overwhelming. This may need additional consideration and bespoke planning/provision within the classroom, and within your school.

Table 11.1 Summary of how to recognise and support need after ABI

Area of need after ABI	What you might notice in the classroom	Tools/adaptations that might help
Fatigue	• Looking dazed or lost, drifting off • Yawning and looking physically pale/grey • More difficulty in regulating emotions and behaviour • Physical skills may become poorer (e.g. handwriting/balance) and some learners struggle to produce or find words and speak clearly • Struggling to follow what is being said • Unable to take in information and make sense of it • Poor recall of previously familiar information • Getting lost part way through an activity	• Be proactive rather than reactive to fatigue • Encourage/facilitate regular 'brain breaks' when cognitive demands are reduced as much as possible • Recognise key contributors to fatigue and try not to have too many at one time – intersperse 'red/brain drain' activities with 'green' restorative activities • Support learners to prioritise and pace • Remember participation is not just learning! • Remember you might not be able to see fatigue, it is likely something you will interpret through observed engagement, emotions, or behaviour
Emotions and behaviour	• Changes in engagement • Low self-esteem • Outbursts of frustration/anger • Increased anxiety • Changes in personality, e.g. impulsivity, disinhibition • Increasingly withdrawn/quiet • Unable to attend/sit still in the classroom	• Take time to talk to the learners and the team about potential triggers and reinforcers • Provide clear boundaries – consistent across staff, setting, activity, and home if possible • Encourage breaks and time away from any sources of frustration • Think about the role of fatigue • Consider introducing some relaxation/grounding exercises • Think about how to support/ build emotional and behavioural regulation skills., e.g. Zones of Regulation

(Continued)

Table 11.1 (Continued)

Area of need after ABI	What you might notice in the classroom	Tools/adaptations that might help
		• Support them to reduce avoidance when they are anxious • Create opportunities for positive reinforcement – activities to boost self-esteem • Take time to connect with strengths and skills that celebrate the learner beyond their acquired needs and injury • Ensure the learner has agency over decisions being made to support them
Executive functions	• Can be disorganised or forgetful • Have trouble getting started on tasks and get distracted easily • Can become angry when routines are changed or expectations not met • Act without realising the consequences of their actions • Continue to engage in unhelpful strategies or behaviours and needing support to shift • School performance can be affected by lost papers or assignments, forgotten homework, last minute work, and careless mistakes • Don't know how to begin long-term assignments • Workspaces, desks, and backpacks resemble 'black holes'. • Emotional outbursts are common	• Allow the learners time to think, plan, and set goals • Help them to recognise their emotions and learn strategies and planned methods for how to cope with them, e.g. taking time-out • Teach tasks in slow, repetitive, step-by-step fashion – tick off each stage when complete • Encourage them to talk about situations and events, and consider different people's views • Help them think up alternatives when an initial plan does not work, or they get stuck. They will probably need step-by-step support in doing this as trial-and-error learning may not be effective • Support them to initiate the use of strategies and monitor their own performance

(Continued)

Table 11.1 (Continued)

Area of need after ABI	What you might notice in the classroom	Tools/adaptations that might help
Processing speed	• Take longer to encode, understand, and use information • Have trouble with reasoning tasks • Get left behind in class • Struggle to follow instructions • Trouble keeping up in all aspects of school, e.g. social situations, learning, daily tasks	• Reduction of unnecessary/surplus tasks • Regular breaks to allow their brain time to 'catch up' • Time allowances (assessment, learning, and homework) • Well-established and understood routines • Appropriate pace of teaching (with check-ins) • Opportunities for increased access to lesson content, e.g. pre-learning, keywords, handouts
Memory	• Trouble with remembering visual things, e.g. places, pictures, diagrams (visual memory) • Trouble with remembering verbal information they have heard, e.g. instructions, names, facts (verbal memory) • Difficulty holding information in mind for a brief time to do something with it, e.g. instructions, arithmetic (working memory)	• Repeat information as much as possible and provide opportunities for pre-learning, rehearsal, and review • Chunk information – i.e. offer information in small amounts, and ensure the learner has remembered/processed before giving the next part • Break down more complex tasks and instructions, and to be given clear step-by-step guidance within learning • Allow learner to take 'brain breaks' within their learning • Give them information in both or preferred verbal and visual formats, e.g. write down instructions, use verbal reminders, use visual prompts • Use recognition memory, e.g. offer prompts and cues to assist recall • Try 'errorless' (error reduced!) learning strategies

Self-reflection

- What could you do to increase ABI awareness and preparedness?
- Do you have a school policy for ABI?
- Do all staff have a shared understanding of the needs of any learners in school with ABI?
- Do you ask families to notify you of any illnesses/injuries that occur over school holidays so that you can monitor them?
- How are learners supported in their return to school after an ABI?

Check out the free online training and resources for teachers around ABI (see resources).

5 top tips

1. Be mindful of the fact that brains develop and change, and this means brain injuries are dynamic/evolving. Consider the learners needs as a whole.
2. Understanding ABI is crucial for all teachers. Learners with ABI may need you to be the detective and the identifier of their history of ABI and its impact on their functioning.
3. Teachers are building brains every day, and this is exactly what learners with ABI need to help them recover, rehabilitate, and compensate for new needs.
4. The usual support tools for your learner cohort may be adequate, but some individualised adaptations around fatigue and the cumulative impact of the ABI may be required. Learning in the classroom can impact fatigue, and learners may appear to be managing (learners with ABI are often good maskers!), but there may be a cumulative impact of their performance at school, on their capacity to

find the energy for skills outside of the classroom, e.g. social skills, leisure, home.
5. Don't forget participation; helping learners to recognise and build their strengths and to be fully included in all aspects of school makes a huge difference to outcomes.

References

Amram, O., Schuurman, N., Pike, I., Yanchar, N.L., Friger, M., McBeth, P.B. & Griesdale, D. (2015). *Socio economic status and traumatic brain injury amongst pediatric populations: A spatial analysis in greater Vancouver.* International Journal of Environmental Research and Public Health, 12(12), pp. 15594–15604.

Bennett, E., Thomas, S. & Woolf, E. (2022). *Childhood acquired brain injury: The knowledge and training needs of special educational needs coordinators.* Support for Learning, 37(2), pp. 209–224.

Cooke, J.E., Deneault, A., Devereux, C., Eirish, R., Pasco Fearon, R.M. & Madigan, S. (2022). *Parental sensitivity and child behavioral problems: A meta-analytic review.* Child Development, 93(5), pp. 1231–1248. DOI: 10.1111/cdev.13764.

Forsyth, R. & Kirkham, F. (2012). *Predicting outcome after childhood brain injury.* Cmaj, 184(11), pp. 1257–1264.

Gracey, F., Watson, S., McHugh, M., Swan, A., Humphrey, A. & Adlam, A. (2014). *Age at injury, emotional problems and executive functioning in understanding disrupted social relationships following childhood acquired brain injury.* Social Care and Neurodisability, 5(3), pp. 160–170.

Hammill, N. Bennett, E. & White, P. (2019). *Making and maintaining a successful return to education after acquired brain injury ('The Sam White Pathway').* Nottinghamshire County Council and Nottingham Children's Hospital. Available from: https://www.nuh.nhs.uk/clinical-psychology-and-neuropsychology

Howe, J. & Ball, H. (2017). *An exploratory study of Special Educational Needs Co-ordinators' knowledge and experience of working with children who have sustained a brain injury.* Support for Learning, 32(1), pp. 85–100.

Jim, J., Costello, G., Lowing, V., Nash, S., Scholes, C., & Perkins, A. (2022). Hidden social inequalities in paediatric neurorehabilitation. In *Systemic approaches to brain injury treatment*. Routledge, pp. 69–87.

Limond, J, Adlam, A.L. & Cormack, M. (2014). *A model for pediatric neurocognitive interventions: considering the role of development and maturation in rehabilitation planning*. Clinical Neuropsychol, 28(2) pp.181–198.

Linden, M.A., Braiden, H.J. & Miller, S. (2013). *Educational professionals' understanding of childhood traumatic brain injury*. Brain Injury, 27(1), pp. 92–102.

McCarron, R.H., Watson, S. & Gracey, F. (2019). *What do kids with acquired brain injury want? Mapping neuropsychological rehabilitation goals to the International Classification of Functioning, Disability and Health*. Journal of the International Neuropsychological Society, 25(4), pp. 403–412.

Todis, B. & Glang, A. (2008). *Redefining success: Results of a qualitative study of postsecondary transition outcomes for youth with traumatic brain injury*. The Journal of Head Trauma Rehabilitation, 23(4), pp. 252–263.

Williams, W.H., Cordan, G., Mewse, A.J., Tonks, J. & Burgess, C.N. (2010 Dec). *Self-reported traumatic brain injury in male young offenders: a risk factor for re-offending, poor mental health and violence?* Neuropsycholo Rehabil. 20(6) pp. 801–812.

Managing medicines in educational settings

Nirusha Govender

Introduction

There is no standardised approach to managing medicines safely and effectively in schools, leading to national variations on how this is being delivered. There are even significant differences in localised areas where some schools experience full collaborative working between themselves, the local authority, and healthcare partners and other schools having little or no support at all with the need to fund all their own healthcare support.

With the above in mind, this chapter aims to provide you with overarching key guidance, strategies, and best practice considerations to support the safe and effective management of medicines in your schools. Specific details relating to the administration of medicines for a child should be contained on the child's Individual Healthcare Plan (see Chapter 3).

Why is managing medicines important for schools?

The number of dispensed prescriptions for learners has increased in recent years, and more learners need to take medicines during school time for a range of medical conditions including asthma, epilepsy, diabetes, attention deficit hyperactivity disorder (ADHD), and other complex health conditions.

The responsibilities of governing bodies of maintained schools, proprietors of academies, and management committees of learner referral units (PRUs) to have a duty to have in place arrangements to support learners with medical conditions at their school is outlined in Chapter 2.

DOI: 10.4324/9781003478942-14

What are the specific challenges of managing medication in schools?

Increasing numbers of learners attending schools have recognised learning disabilities and physical and/or mental health conditions, with many having complex health and care needs. This may include the requirement to administer medicines (sometimes off-label or unlicensed – see Glossary) with complex dosing regimens in specific conditions or when managing acute episodes, e.g. during a seizure or asthma attack. This may also include medicines administered via specialist devices, e.g. intrathecal pumps, enteral feeding tubes, infusion pumps, and syringe drivers (see Glossary).

Most schools do not employ a school nurse, so teaching staff play a significant role in medicines administration, storage, and other healthcare-related matters during school hours. These individuals, without access to appropriate training and support, may lack medical or pharmaceutical experience and confidence to carry out this role. Parents can worry when sending their child to school if they need medicines during the school day and an associated anxiety for staff if they do not feel confident in administering them. The paper by Smith et al. (2008) identified medication-related issues from the perspective of young people and their parents, indicating ways in which their needs might be served more sensitively and effectively and is a useful reference.

What can you do in terms of legislation/good practice?

In this section we aim to provide you with a comprehensive guide to the key areas that need to be considered when managing medicines safely in your school as well as support you to ensure that your school can implement best practice.

Policy development

There are several different pieces of legislation covered in Chapter 1 that set out the legal requirements for the handling and administration of medicines in schools, which includes a requirement for a policy that clearly outlines the roles and responsibilities of all staff involved with medicines management. Further information can be found in Chapter 2. More specifically, in terms of this area, the policy must include:

- Specific staff roles and responsibilities in relation to managing learners' medical needs and medicines in school.
- The school's policy on administering non-prescription/over the counter (OTC) medicines.
- How medicines should be delivered to and stored in school.
- How learners and staff access medicines.
- Whether learners are permitted to keep any medicine with them during the school day, e.g. inhalers for asthma when a child can self-administer medicines.
- Record-keeping in relation to medicines.
- Medicines audits, checks, and incident reporting process.
- What to do in the event of a learner becoming seriously unwell.
- What to do in the event of a learner having an adverse reaction to medicines.
- What learning will be undertaken from serious incidents or near misses to improve processes.

If you have an existing relationship or access to local healthcare partners, then it is advisable to work with the specialist health teams (e.g. community children's nursing teams or specialist pharmacy teams) to develop your local policy for medicines administration with associated standard operating procedures (SOPs), as research from Bellis et al. (2017) shows the differences between how individual schools manage medicines and interpret policy guidance and discrepancies between the views of each stakeholder group, with some evidence that medicines management does not always meet the needs of learners and their families.

There are digital software tools available to support you with templates to use in association with your policy, and further details can be found in the resources. They are available for:

- Parental/Carer Consent for Medicines Administration.
- Medicines Administration Record Chart.

- Medicines Administration Record for School Trips.
- Medicines Optimisation Audit Tool Checklist.
- Medicines Optimisation Medicines Incident/Near Miss Record.
- Letters to Community Pharmacy for School Emergency Medicines support (salbutamol and adrenaline).

Please also refer to Chapter 2 on the development of your policy.

Self-reflection

- Do you have a policy for the administration of medication in school?
- Use the lists above to check that you have included all you need to in your policy.

Consent

You must have parental/carer consent to administer any medicines, including both prescription and non-prescription (that is over the counter [OTC] medicines that can be purchased in a community pharmacy or other retail environment).

Written consent is required from a parent/carer before you give a child under 16 any medicine. This must be kept within the child's records and renewed with parents/carers for each new academic year as a minimum or sooner as appropriate.

There are some 'exceptional circumstances' when the medicine has been prescribed without the knowledge of a parent/carer (e.g. contraceptive medicine). In this case, encourage the learner to involve a parent/carer whilst respecting their right to confidentiality.

The consent form must include specific information about the medicines including the name, dose, time, method of administration, and any special instructions. You may wish to use the written consent to also document the agreement for how the medicines will be delivered to your school, e.g. that the medicines will be handed to a specific member of staff or, in the case of emergency medication, it will always be available with the child attached to their wheelchair in a bumbag with the emergency plan.

As well as written consent from the parent/carer, staff should seek verbal consent from the learner before administering medicine where appropriate. Some learners may not like taking medicines, so talking to them beforehand and agreeing a method can avoid difficulties administering the medication, e.g. having a drink ready for the learner to have afterwards to help deal with any unpleasant taste.

Seeking consent and promoting the learner's independence as much as possible is likely to make the process easier for both the learner and staff member and help to avoid issues such as learners spitting medicine out which can be more common with younger learners.

Parent/carer partnership

Parents/carers play a fundamental role in ensuring their child's safety and well-being during the administration of their medication in school. Collaboration and co-production on a learner's Individual Healthcare Plan are key (see Chapter 3). Partnerships with parents/carers will facilitate:

- The provision of accurate and up-to-date information about their child's medical needs and medicines requirements.
- Effective communication with your staff relating to any medicine changes for their child.
- Your staff feeding back questions to parents/carers and identifying challenges with medicines use in the school setting.
- Collaboration with you to develop a robust process for the safe administration of medicines to their child.

There are numerous ways your staff could stay connected with parents/carers about medicines in schools, including emails (generic or targeted), school newsletters, school website, and closed parent platforms or applications (apps), phone calls, and letters.

As collaboration and co-production is a two-way continuous process with parents/carers, you will be able to create a safe and secure environment to support medicines administration.

Staff training

All schools must support learners with medical conditions under the Children and Families Act (2014). This will help keep learners healthy and safe. Medicines must be given safely and professionally with an understanding of basic medical awareness. With more learners needing medicines support, professional training can make a significant difference.

Clarification of who is responsible and who is accountable for administration of medication is important and should be contained within your policy. Please note that there is no legal requirement for a teacher to administer medicines.

The headteacher of your school is accountable for administration of medicines, accepting responsibility or liability for the outcome of your actions. However, staff must be able to explain and give reasons for their actions and decisions and will be accountable for the outcome of any actions they take which were not in line with the school policy or the training they have received.

Identified staff will have the responsibility of carrying out a defined set of tasks or functions and conducting those tasks to the best of their ability, in line with school policy. Being responsible for handling and administering medicines means that a staff member must have some knowledge of the procedures required and so must be trained and supervised until competent. As identified staff members have a responsibility for administering medicines, they are accountable for the outcome of this process and should not delegate the task to other staff members who may not be trained or competent.

The importance of accountability for medicines handling and administration means staff are responsible for only carrying out tasks they have been trained to, following the school's policies and procedures. Staff members are responsible for keeping their knowledge up-to-date, never conducting tasks they are not trained in, being aware of the limitation of any training they have undertaken, and reporting any concerns.

There are several training providers delivering bespoke training either through e-Learning modules or face-to-face training for medicines awareness in schools with varying costs. There are both private companies and healthcare partners that may be able to provide the relevant training to your organisation. With healthcare partners, you may have a nurse or pharmacist/pharmacy technician deliver such training.

Once training has been completed, staff involved with medicines administration must be supported with competency assessments with regular updates and reviews of competence. It is advisable to undertake the training annually as a minimum requirement and undertake regular competency assessments in accordance with the individual staff member's needs.

By completing medicines administration training, staff members can develop their knowledge and confidence, their understanding of the procedures to safely administer medicines, and how to significantly minimise the risk of medicines errors. Being able to administer medicines safely and effectively in emergency situations, e.g. during an asthma attack or a seizure, can prevent a learner from becoming significantly unwell and can even save lives. Having good training in place and robust policies and procedures ensures that your environment is accessible and inclusive and there are reduced barriers to learners with medical conditions when accessing learning.

It is important to ensure that whichever training provider is used, they can meet the required objectives for medicines training and offer a bespoke package relevant to, and suitable for, educational settings.

Here are a few suggested learning outcomes that any medicines management in schools training should cover as a minimum, but it is also advisable to seek advice from your local healthcare partners or medicines specialist, e.g. community children's nurse, school nurse, or a pharmacist.

- Identification of the different legal categories of medicines.
- How to find information about individual medicines.
- Understanding of staff responsibilities in the safe management of medicines at school.
- Understanding the importance of policies and standard operating procedures relating to medicines.
- Administering medicines safely and effectively.
- Record management: use and maintaining appropriate school documentation records.
- Incident/near miss reporting: recognise and avoid potential problems with medicines.
- Understand the side-effects of medicines.
- Know how to dispose of medicines waste safely and correctly.

Self-reflection

- Are your staff involved in administration of medication appropriately trained and confident to carry out their role?
- Are your recording processes and procedures adequate?
- How do you engage with parents to ensure that you are working collaboratively?

Storage of medicines

You can only administer medicine (both prescription and non-prescription) which are supplied to you in its original container and clearly labelled. For prescription medicine, the label must have been printed by the dispensing pharmacy with the following information:

- Medicine's name, strength, and formulation.
- Child's name and details.
- Date of issue from pharmacy.
- Dosage.
- Administration instructions.
- Expiry date.
- Storage instructions.

Similarly, your staff can only administer non-prescription medicines that are supplied in the original container with manufacturer's guidance for administration.

Any medicines received which do not meet these requirements would usually be returned to the parent/carer so any issues can be rectified, e.g. incomplete dispensing label with a dosage instruction of 'As directed'. Medicines which do not meet the requirements of the school policy should not be kept on the premises.

If a medicine is presented to you in line with your policy and has been accepted, the next step is to store it appropriately. Appropriate storage of

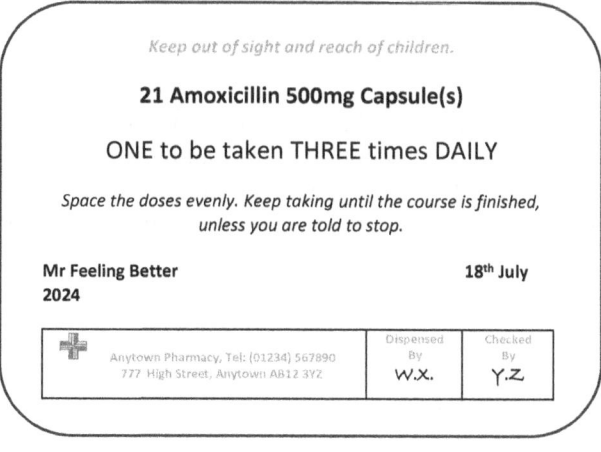

Figure 12.1 Example of prescription medicine, and the information that should be contained on the label printed by the dispensing pharmacy

medicines in line with the manufacturer's instructions is crucial to maintain their effectiveness and prevent tampering.

You should follow best practices for safe storage, including:

- Storing medicine in an appropriate place. This may be a secure, locked area with controlled access such as a locked cupboard in the classroom which is secure but easily accessible by designated staff who are trained and authorised to administer medicines.
- Maintaining proper temperature and humidity conditions in line with instructions for each medicine. Note, most medicines (unless stated otherwise) can be stored at room temperature. These products are usually labelled 'do not store above 25°C' (or for some products 'do not store above 30°C'). Some products can be irreversibly damaged by even brief periods outside of the stated storage conditions (most notably vaccines and liquid antibiotics require storage in a fridge between 2 and 8°C). As a matter of good practice, monitoring room temperature where medicines cupboards are situated is recommended.
- Having a robust recording mechanism for audit trail purposes to manage medicines supplies in and out of school.

- Storing medicines in their original containers including pharmacy dispensing labels for prescription medicines.
- Not storing medicines correctly increases the probability of an incident occurring. It can also affect the efficacy and stability of the medicine which can put the learner at risk.

In summary, the minimum best practice requirements for the safe storage and administration of medicines in your school are as follows:

- Only accept medicines in unopened, original bottles or packaging.
- All medicines must be clearly labelled with the learner's details.
- Consent forms must be completed by parents/carers for all medicines (including over-the-counter medicine, such as painkillers).
- Prescribed medicines should have a printed label from the dispensing pharmacy.
- Medicine must be stored as per the original instructions in a suitable area with limited access by authorised staff members.
- Staff administering medicines should receive training and be assessed as competent by a senior lead for health.
- You must act in line with legislation and best practice.

Administration of medicines

Administering medicines will always carry a level of risk. Most medicines can be given at intervals which can be planned around the school day, e.g. antibiotics which must be taken three times a day could be given at home before school, after school, and before bedtime.

It is therefore reasonable for you to collaborate with parents/carers and healthcare professionals to see whether the medicines can be administered outside of school hours.

So, medicines should only be administered during school hours when it is absolutely necessary and the medicine cannot be given before/ after school, e.g. time critical medicines that must be given at specific dosing intervals during the day or medicines crucial to support the management of health condition symptoms as they occur during the course of the day.

Before staff can administer any medicine to learners, there are several checks which need to take place. These checks are referred to as "The 5 Rights +1" or "The 6 Rights":

1. Right learner
2. Right medicine
3. Right time
4. Right dose
5. Right route
   +1 Right documentation.

All of which are regarded as a standard for safe medicines practices.

When agreeing to administer a non-prescription/OTC medicine, you should be reassured that you are not making the clinical decision that the medicine is appropriate for the child's health condition. This responsibility remains with the parent and/or carer following their written consent. No child under 16 should be given non-prescription/OTC medicines without their parent's and/or carer's written consent.

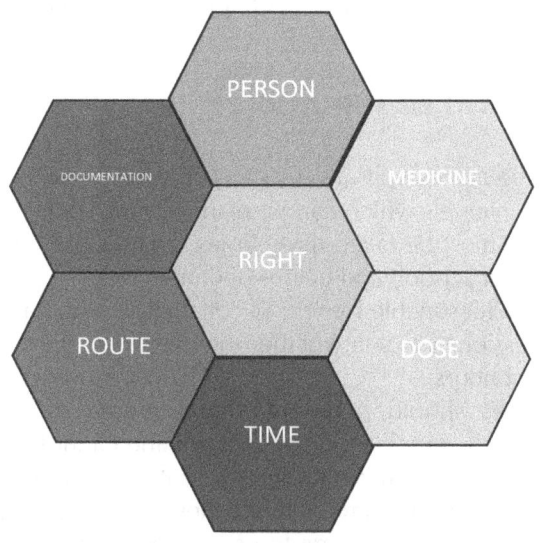

Figure 12.2 "The 5 Rights +1" or "The 6 Rights" when administering medication

A Medicines Administration Record (MAR) chart is the record that shows medicines that have been administered to a learner. The staff member signs each time a medicine is administered to a learner. Staff members administrating medicines should be suitably trained in how to use MAR charts and undertake regular refresher training.

Producing MAR charts should be undertaken by healthcare professionals, e.g. school nurses or community pharmacies. However, if your school does not have access to local healthcare services and needs to produce your own MAR charts, then you must ensure you work to the Royal Pharmaceutical Society standards for writing MAR charts (see References).

A MAR chart must not be produced by teaching staff unless they have been trained and competently assessed in transcribing medicines. This role should be reserved for a limited number of staff members who have received additional training by a suitably qualified health professional.

Legislation for the administering of medicines in schools outlines the following roles and responsibilities:

- Parents/carers have the primary responsibility for their child's health and well-being.
- Your governing body is responsible for ensuring learners with medical conditions are supported and have access to a full education.
- Your headteacher is responsible for ensuring that policies are implemented, and all staff are aware of the policy and their role in relation to supporting learners with medical needs.
- Your staff must ensure learners are supported to access and take medicines safely when it is needed during school hours.
- Your teachers do not have a legal or contractual duty to administer or supervise learners taking medicines; however, they can take on this role voluntarily.
- Any staff member involved in administering medicines is responsible for ensuring they follow the school's policies and procedures when carrying out this role.

Further information can be found in the research paper by Wong et al. (2004), and more information about who is responsible for administering medicines can be found in the paper by Bannon and Ross (1998). Bannon and Ross provide the best statement which provides some directive to support headteachers in this challenging environment.

> *The complex legal framework (which includes the Health and Safety at Work Act 1974, the Medicines Act 1968, and the Education Act 1993) is interpreted. The conclusion is that there is no legal duty requiring school staff to administer drugs to children, which remains a voluntary role. The term 'in loco parentis' is obsolete and is not relevant in this context. However, school staff who oversee children have a duty in common law to act in the same manner as a responsible parent in order to ensure that learners remain safe and healthy while on school premises. In certain circumstances teachers might be expected to administer drugs or to take appropriate action in an emergency.*

Learner self-administration of medicines

Allowing learners to do as much as possible of the medicine administration process for themselves will support them to become more responsible and independent in managing their own medicines. For learners with long-term medical conditions, this can be important for building their level of self-confidence and sense of responsibility for their own well-being.

Learners should be actively encouraged to take responsibility for the administration of their own medicines if they are competent to do so. This is particularly beneficial in urgent situations requiring emergency medicines, such as adrenaline devices and asthma inhalers, as the learner can administer their own medication.

Where appropriate, learners should be allowed to be in charge of their own medicines, either keeping them securely on their person or in lockable facilities they can access. It is advisable for a risk assessment to be considered and completed to minimise the potential for harm to occur.

It is critical to work with parents/carers to see if/how self-administration works at home and see if/how this can be replicated at school. Care needs to be taken with neurodiverse learners, and consultation with parents/carers in this situation is particularly important.

Vulnerable learners may require a more bespoke approach to the management of medicines in school with the support of a multi-disciplinary approach and the development of an Individual Healthcare Plan. The paper by Gray et al. (2022) outlines more information about the benefits of self-management of medicines by learners with medical conditions in schools.

Managing medical emergencies in school

The Department for Education guidance (2014) states that it is reasonable for all school staff to be trained to recognise the signs and symptoms of emergency situations. A learner's Individual Healthcare Plan may identify the need for some staff to have further information about a medical condition or specific training in administering a particular type of medicine, including dealing with emergencies.

Additional training courses such as Paediatric First Aid and First Aid at Work is required and will provide the knowledge and skills to be able to deal with emergency medical situations including, but not limited to:

- Asthma attacks.
- Anaphylaxis and allergic reactions.
- Epileptic seizures.
- Hypoglycaemia – low blood sugar.
- Cardiopulmonary resuscitation (CPR).

These courses are certificated and require refresher training to be undertaken to maintain competency and certification. Further specialist training from healthcare partners, e.g. specialist epilepsy nurse, will be needed by any staff who are required to administer medicines for epileptic seizures.

The most common rescue medicines in schools include:

- Buccal midazolam, e.g. Buccolam Oromucosal Solution and rectal diazepam for epilepsy.
- Adrenaline auto-injectors, e.g. EpiPen® or Jext® pens for anaphylactic/allergic reactions.
- Blue salbutamol reliever inhalers, e.g. Ventolin® evohalers for asthma attacks.
- Glucose or dextrose tablets or gel, e.g. Glucogel® for hypoglycaemia (low blood sugar) typically associated with diabetes.

Learners who require rescue medicines for asthma, epilepsy, and anaphylaxis should have an emergency medicines action plan. It is recommended that the emergency medicine along with the action plan are always kept with the child in a secure but accessible manner. Some schools develop a standardised approach and use bumbags that are kept with the child all day, in learners' school bags, or attached to wheelchairs. There are some commercially available, e.g. from Medpac (see Resources).

Lives can be saved if staff are able to recognise the signs and symptoms of a medical emergency in your school so they can give immediate medical assistance before professional medical help arrives. By starting treatment right away, you can prevent the condition from worsening before expert care arrives. Providing this immediate, possibly life-saving medical care is vital in ensuring the learner's safety either before further medical help arrives, or before taking the learner to the hospital, should this be required.

Managing medication in schools: legislative changes to support schools

Management of asthma in schools

From 1 October 2014, UK schools have been allowed to purchase a salbutamol inhaler without a prescription for use in emergencies when a learner with asthma cannot access their own inhaler. 'Guidance on the use of emergency salbutamol inhalers in schools' (Department of Health, 2015) will give you the choice to keep an emergency inhaler on the basis of creating a policy or protocol for using it (see Resources).

Use of adrenaline auto-injectors (commonly known brands: EpiPen® or Jext® pens) in schools

From 1 October 2017, schools in England have been allowed to purchase adrenaline auto-injector (AAI) devices without a prescription, for emergency use on learners who are at risk of anaphylaxis but whose own device is not available or not working. 'Guidance on the use of adrenaline auto-injectors in schools' (2017), issued by the Department of Health, will help you to choose whether to keep an emergency AAI and create a policy for using it (see Resources). There is also a link to the spare pens in school website for managing anaphylaxis in the online resources.

Most community pharmacies should have an awareness of the above guidelines for holding additional emergency supplies in schools. You should be able to purchase these items from a community pharmacy.

Please note that the staff responsible for making the purchase on behalf of the school may be required to provide appropriate identification or bring a signed letter from the headteacher on school-headed paper to provide assurance to the community pharmacy when making the purchase.

What to do if you make a medicines error

There are many ways to minimise the risk of a medicines error occurring, but they can still occur. A medicines error is any patient safety incident where there has been an error while:

- prescribing
- preparing
- dispensing
- administering
- monitoring
- providing advice on medicines.

Medicines errors are not the same as adverse drug reactions. Medicines errors occur when weak medicines systems or human factors affect processes, and human factors that my influence errors in a school setting include factors such as fatigue, environmental conditions, and staffing levels.

Any medicines errors can lead to minor symptoms/reactions or could have serious consequences and result in severe harm, disability, or death.

Some examples of medicines errors include:

- Missed dose: forgetting to administer a medicine.
- Giving the wrong medicine.
- Giving too much or too little of a medicine.
- Giving a medicine the wrong way (i.e. via the wrong route).
- Giving medicine at the wrong time.

If a staff member makes a medicines error, they must never ignore it or try to cover it up. This will lead to more harm to the learner and more profound consequences for the staff member and the school.

Your school's medicines policy must contain a clear procedure for staff to follow should a medicines error occur. Staff should be supported and encouraged to be open and transparent when it comes to errors, so the focus should be on what they can do to prevent a more serious situation developing, rather than a blame culture.

Learning and sharing best practice to improve processes in school are also recommended to support the non-blame culture and continuous learning approach. A positive approach to learning from medicines errors and sharing best practice improvements can lead to enhanced efficiency to medicines management processes and strengthening and empowering co-production relationships with learners and parents/carers and support an overall positive culture within the school.

Self-reflection

- Do you keep asthma pumps and adrenaline auto-injectors in your school?
- Do you know where they are kept and who is responsible to ensure they are in date and used appropriately?
- Does your school have an open culture where staff feel safe to admit if they have made a medicines error? If the answer is no, how can you change this?

Access to medicines information for schools, learners, and parents/carers

Medicines information today is easily accessible through the touch of a button on the World Wide Web, so it is important to ensure that you and your staff access medicines information from reputable and accredited sources in the UK.

The electronic Medicines Compendium (eMC) from Datapharm (2024) provides a range of useful and accurate information, which is added to the site by the pharmaceutical manufacturers. The eMC provides two main types of information:

- Summaries of Product Characteristics (SmPCs), which provide a summary of the technical information associated with a medicine which is more suitable for use by healthcare professionals.
- Patient information leaflets (PILs), which provide a more 'user friendly' version of the information found in SmPCs which is more suitable for use by the general public.

For many people, the primary or only source of information about their medicine is the statutory patient information leaflets (PILs) which, since 1999, have had to be supplied with all medicines. These provide the essential information which people need to enable them to use medicines safely and gain the most benefit. Unlike other sources of information, the PIL is highly regulated. All PILs are required to be reviewed and approved by the Medicines and Healthcare products Regulatory Agency (MHRA) before being supplied with the medicine. The information which is provided within the PIL is set out in European and national legislation. All pharmacies who dispense prescription medicines must include a PIL at the point of supply. Similarly, all OTC medicines must contain a PIL provided by the manufacturer in its original packaging.

Many medicines prescribed for use in learners with more complex heath needs are often 'off-label' or 'unlicensed' (see Glossary), e.g. when administering medicines via enteral feeding tubes. In this case, all stakeholders require information about medicines, and a good resource for you to become familiar with is the accredited Medicines for Learners website (2024), which is run in partnership by three UK-based organisations focussed on child health – the Royal College of Paediatrics and Child Health (RCPCH), the Neonatal Paediatric Pharmacist Group (NPPG), and the children's charity WellChild®.

This website provides useful leaflets for patients and carers covering:

- How to give medicines – practical tips for different dosage forms.
- Specific medicines – including information on side-effects and advice on what to do if the child vomits or a dose is missed.

- General medicines advice – such as travelling with medicines and information about unlicensed medicines and off-label use.

Making use of your local pharmacist

Improving health and well-being and helping to reduce health inequalities are major priorities for a community pharmacy. Pharmacists' skills of listening, explaining, advising, and questioning are all highly relevant to help identify and support the medicines management needs of learners with complex health needs in schools. With an increasing number of learners with these needs requiring medicines to be administered at school, school staff are encouraged to collaborate not only with parents/carers and healthcare professionals, but also with their local community pharmacy. This is to ensure that only medicines that are essential for the learner need to be administered in school. Community pharmacists are local, accessible, and ideally placed to develop close links with learners, their families, and schools. They can support you in:

- Safe and effective management of medicines to learners in your school to minimise the risk of errors through medicines reviews and the provision of MAR charts if appropriate.
- Effectively managing the supply of medicines for long-term medical conditions in learners, improving monthly repeat prescription management and minimising waste.
- Accessing medicines information and answering questions related to individual learners' medication needs from parents/carers.
- Promoting a more localised approach to quality improvement initiatives around medicines safety at home and in schools.

Where possible and appropriate to do so, consult with parents/carers and healthcare professionals to obtain separate prescriptions for the supply of medicines for home and school. This will enable you to receive a unique supply that is correctly labelled for the duration of the school term. This may be particularly useful in boarding/residential schools.

Collaborate with parents/carers, healthcare partners, and local community pharmacies to ensure medicines can be safely managed in your school.

Community pharmacies also provide access to medicines information and resources including leaflets, dispensing labels, and medicines-related advice for parents and schools, including advice and support on:

- Medicines administration and dosing intervals.
- Medicines administered via specialist medical devices including enteral feeding tubes, infusion pumps, intrathecal pumps, and syringe drivers.
- Special storage instructions for specific medicines where appropriate.
- Emergency medicines at school for asthma and anaphylaxis.
- Advising on off-label and unlicensed use of medicines when appropriate.

Self-reflection

- Do you know who in your learner cohorts need to have medication administered during the school day?
- Do you use MAR charts?
- Have you liaised with your pharmacy, specialist community nurses, school nurses, and local authority personnel to support you in managing medication in your school?

5 top tips

1. Ensure you have a lead for health in place to support the development of the medicines policy and associated SOPs including processes to manage the administration of emergency medicines.

2. Ensure all staff responsible for the administration of medicines have annual training from suitably qualified healthcare professionals and have a regular review of their competence to administer medicines safely.
3. Collaborate with key healthcare professionals (including community pharmacies) as part of a multi-disciplinary approach to ensure only essential medicines are administered in school.
4. Ensure there is a robust record and audit trail of the medicines administration whether via bespoke software or MAR charts.
5. Ensure all medicines-related errors, incidents, and near misses are recorded, and the lessons learnt are shared as part of continuing professional development with all staff.

Glossary

Acute illness/condition
An acute condition is typically defined as a disease, illness, or injury that is likely to respond quickly to treatment and aims to return the person to the state of health they were in immediately before suffering the condition, or which leads to a full recovery.

Enteral feeding tubes
Enteral nutrition (EN) is a type of tube-feeding for nutritional support. EN is where the nutritional fluid or feed is given into the gut, through a tube going into the stomach or small intestine. EN works best if your digestive system is working normally but you are not able to eat or drink enough.

A Percutaneous Endoscopic Gastrostomy (PEG) feeding tube insertion is the placement of a feeding tube through the skin and the stomach wall. It goes directly into the stomach. PEG feeding tube insertion is done in part using a procedure called endoscopy. Feeding tubes are needed when a person is unable to eat or drink to allow liquid feed, medicines, and water to be passed into the stomach.

Infusion pumps

An infusion device is a small machine that makes sure the drugs or fluids prescribed by a doctor are infused smoothly and accurately into the body. Infusion pumps are designed to be highly accurate and precise, with the ability to deliver very small amounts of fluid over a long period of time. They are often used to deliver medications or fluids at a constant rate, or to deliver them in a specific pattern.

Intrathecal pumps

An implantable intrathecal pump is a medical device used to deliver very small quantities of medications to the spinal fluid. For example, medicines such as morphine or baclofen are delivered in this manner to minimise the side-effects associated with oral medications.

Syringe drivers

A syringe driver is a small battery-powered pump. It delivers medications through a small tube or needle just under the patient's skin (subcutaneously) usually over a 24-hour period. Syringe drivers are commonly used for symptom management and are used to provide continuous medications subcutaneously when a person is no longer able to swallow.

Unlicensed medicines and 'off-label' use

What is a medicine?

Medicines are products used to prevent or treat a medical condition. They come in many forms, for example tablets, liquids, injections, creams, eye drops, etc.

Licensing of medicines

In the UK, medicines need to have a licence before they can be widely used.

To get a licence, the manufacturer of the medicine must provide evidence that shows that the medicine works well enough and is safe enough to be used for a specific condition and for a specific group of patients, and that they can manufacture the medicine to the required quality. A drug company must have a product licence, sometimes known as a Marketing Authorisation, to advertise and sell a medicine. The licence states which illness the medicine can be used for, how much can be used, how to give the medicine, and which group of patients it can be given to. The licence is provided by a government organisation in the UK called the Medicines and Healthcare products Regulatory Agency, also known as MHRA.

Medicines can be prescribed if they do not have a licence (**unlicensed**) or for **'off-label'** use.

Off-label means that the person prescribing the medicine wants to use it in a different way than that stated in its licence. This could mean using the medicine for a different condition or a different group of patients, or it could mean a change in the dose or that the medicine is taken in a different way.

Some examples of 'off-label' uses are:

- Using a medicine for a different illness to that stated in the licence. Doctors may have found that the medicine works very well for this illness or condition. This use may be supported by expert groups, but the drug company has not applied for a license to treat this illness or condition.
- Using a medicine in an age group outside the licensed range (usually learners or the elderly).
- Using a medicine at a higher dose than stated in the licence.

Unlicensed medicines are where:

- A medicine has a licence in other countries, but not the UK. It must be imported because it is not available in the UK.
- The medicine needs to be made up as a special product because it is not readily available. This is often the case for liquid formulations of medicines which only have a license for the tablet form.
- A medicine that has no licence at all. These are often medicines used for treating rare illnesses. The manufacturer may have decided that it was too expensive to carry out the clinical trials or it would be difficult to find enough patients for the clinical trials needed to get a licence.

References

Bannon, M.J. & Ross, E.M. (1998). *Administration of medicines in school: Who is responsible?* The British Medical Journal. Available here: https://www.ncbi.nlm.nih.gov/pmc/articles/PMC1113203/

Bellis, J.R., Arnott, J., Barker, C., Prescott, R., Dray, O., Peak, M. & Bracken, L. (2017). *Medicines in schools: A cross-sectional survey of learners, parents, teachers, and health professionals.* BMJ Paediatrics Open. Available from: https://bmjpaedsopen.bmj.com/content/1/1/e000110 accessed 28.06.24.

Datapharm (2024), *Electronic Medicines Compendium*, Accessed at https://www.medicines.org.uk/emc#gref on 28.08.24.

Department for Education (2014). *Supporting learners with medical conditions at school.* Available here: https://www.gov.uk/government/publications/supporting-learners-at-school-with-medical-conditions--3

Department of Health (2015). *Guidance on the use of emergency salbutamol inhalers in schools.* Available at https://assets.publishing.service.gov.uk/media/5a74eb55ed915d3c7d528f98/emergency_inhalers_in_schools.pdf accessed 28.08.24.

Department of Health (2017). *Guidance on the use of adrenaline auto-injectors in schools.* Available at https://assets.publishing.service.gov.uk/media/5a829e3940f0b6230269bcf4/Adrenaline_auto_injectors_in_schools.pdf accessed on 28.08.24.

Gray, N., Al-Sallami, M., Cunningham, C., Hadi, M., Janowska, N., Lazri, M. & Saleem, F. (2022). *Self-administration of medicines at school by students living with medical conditions.* Developmental and Adolescent Health Journal. Available here: https://pure.hud.ac.uk/en/publications/self-administration-of-medicines-at-school-by-students-living-wit

Royal College of Paediatrics and Child Health (RCPCH), Neonatal Paediatric Pharmacist Group (NPPG) & WellChild® (2024). *Medicines for Learners.* Available at https://www.medicinesforlearners.org.uk/ accessed 26.08.24.

Royal Pharmaceutical Society of Great Britain (2009). *Principles of safe and appropriate production of medicine administration charts.* Available at https://www.rpharms.com/Portals/0/RPS%20document%20library/Open%20access/Hub/production-medicine-administration-charts.pdf accessed 26.08.24.

Smith, F.J., Taylor, K.M.G., Newbould, J. & Keady, S. (2008). *Medicines for chronic illness at school: Experiences and concerns of young people and their parents.* Journal of Clinical Pharmacy & Therapeutics, 33(5), pp. 537–544. Available from: https://pubmed.ncbi.nlm.nih.gov/18834369/

UK Legislation: *Learners and Families Act 2014*, Chapter 6. Available at: https://www.legislation.gov.uk/ukpga/2014/6

Wong, I.C.K., Awolowo, T., Gordon, K. & Mo, Y.W. (2004). *Survey of administration of medicines to learners in primary schools within the London area.* Archives of Disease in Childhood, 89(11) pp. 998–1001. DOI: 10.1136/adc.2003.047258

Best practice in supporting reintegration to school following a period of absence

James Shryane and Victoria Howard

Introduction

In this chapter we are exploring reintegration, i.e. welcoming a child back to their school following a sustained period of absence due to ill health. Typical conditions that prevent learners from attending school for a prolonged period include anxiety, eating disorders, psychosis, and physical health conditions such as cancer or Cystic Fibrosis.

As headteachers of schools for learners with medical needs, our aim is for all our learners to return to their usual school or other long-term provision as soon as their health allows. We have facilitated many reintegrations and hope to share some of this expertise with you to inform your practice. Throughout the chapter we refer to medical alternative provision (AP), but in your area this service may be provided by a hospital school or other local authority commissioned service, including home tuition services.

Access to school is extremely important to all learners from both an academic point of view as well as a social one. All learners deserve the opportunity to be included in their local school community. For learners with medical needs, this will require 'reasonable adjustments' to be made to ensure they can be included alongside their peers. We see learners thrive in the small nurturing environment provided by our medical needs alternative provisions and hospital schools, but we all have a duty to ensure mainstream

DOI: 10.4324/9781003478942-15

schools have the skills and resources to provide an inclusive education to meet the needs of all learners.

Severe and persistent absence has been increasing through the 2020s, and the ecosystem of support has not been able to keep up with the growing problem. The result is that schools have been seeing learners with more complex and entrenched issues, so that reintegration has undoubtedly become more difficult.

Despite these challenges, there are still several practical things that can be done to make reintegration more likely to succeed. We will share some of the good practices that we have encountered during a combined 60 years of working in education and over 20 years working with learners with medical needs.

Self-reflection

- What is your current success rate at reintegrating learners back to your school after a period of absence?
- What barriers and enablers have you noticed?

Practical, cost-effective strategies that can be used in your school

Welcome your learners back to school

Before considering your school's approach to reintegration, it is worth reflecting on the values and beliefs that we all develop over many years in our complex roles working in schools. Ask yourself, 'Am I coming at this with an open mind and with an inclusive approach?' We see a variety of values expressed through the actions of different members of staff in schools that are often coloured by one or more of the challenges schools face, as described in the introduction to this chapter. These include:

- The pressure to improve attendance.
- The pressure of league tables and examination results.
- General challenges of juggling a school budget that is being pulled in many directions at once.

In our experience, the most important thing is that the learner feels you will welcome them back with open arms, you want them back in your school, and you will do whatever is necessary to make the reintegration process work.

Working in partnership

A reintegration is likely to be a piece of partnership working that you undertake alongside your local medical AP. Attending regular reviews will keep you up to date with how the learner is doing academically, how their health condition continues to impact on school, and when they are beginning to show signs that they are ready to reintegrate back to you, their home school.

Telepresence robots are a great way to help the child remain in touch with the learning in their school as well as maintain the social links that are so important. They can also be used as part of the reintegration process. The use of telepresence robots is explored more fully in Chapter 9.

Medical AP staff are highly trained and experienced. They will know the learners as individuals and closely monitor their engagement in education, recognising the small personal gains and growth in resilience which are required to enable a learner to be able to begin their reintegration. Regular contact with medical practitioners, who also work closely with the learners, will indicate when a learner's health has improved sufficiently for them to begin the return to your school. This window of opportunity gives all professionals time to plan, with the learners' voice at the centre of a successful reintegration.

From the very start of a learner's entry into the medical AP, reintegration will always be the intended outcome. The reintegration plan will start with capturing the learners voice, preferences, and desired outcomes.

Capturing the learner's voice

There are many tools to help when doing this, and the best method will depend on the individual child. Examples include:

* *The Three Houses* (https://www.socialworkerstoolbox.com/the-three-houses-template/) often used by social workers

- *Blob Tree* (https://www.blobtree.com/pages/frontpage)
- Other tools available focused on the child's wishes and feelings, including from CAFCASS (see also Chapter 10 and resources) (https://www.voiceofthechild.org.uk/kb/needs-wishes-feelings-guidance-cafcass/).

Your medical AP is likely to use these tools to understand where the child is now.

Gradual exposure and small steps

Once these barriers have been identified, your medical AP will set a series of goals for the learner, and each of these will be broken down into small, achievable steps. For example, the goal of 'getting to the school site', for a learner who is reluctant to leave home, may be split into:

- Getting into the learner's garden.
- Taking a walk around the block.
- Visiting a place where there are other people such as a cafe or library.
- Driving past the school out of hours.
- Driving past the school during the school day.
- Driving to the school car park and remaining in the car.
- Driving to the school car park and exiting the car.

Each of these steps may take several attempts and should not be rushed. You need to trust the expertise of your medical AP and take their advice on the pace of progress. A reduced timetable is likely to form part of the reintegration process. Generally, allow two weeks between each addition to the timetable, as trying to go too fast can result in setbacks. Setting arbitrary time limits on reintegration is counterproductive to success, and psychological theory around behaviour change tells us that relapse is an inevitable part of the process of change. This should be discussed from the start, so that when it happens it is seen as a natural part of the process rather than a sign of failure.

It is important for learners to enter a stressful reintegration situation and leave it with a lowered sense of anxiety. Stop each session while it is going well and resist the temptation to push on beyond what was initially planned. At times, even the learner may want to push themselves further, but extending to a point where anxiety is raised can be counterproductive. Quit while you are ahead!

Reasonable adjustments to rigid school rules may not appear to be reasonable to your school management. They may need convincing that exceptions to the rules are necessary to help the learner successfully reintegrate. Be open to making reasonable adjustments to rules around school uniform, eating, mobile phone use, access to toilets, and start and finish times.

Using an Individual Healthcare Plan

The key to ensuring the learner, family, and school are all confident that a safe and successful reintegration can happen is planning. A good place to start is with the Individual Healthcare Plan (see Chapter 3). This document, first described in the 2014 statutory guidance 'Supporting learners with medical conditions at school' is used to record key contacts and responsibilities, details of support needs, medication, and what to do in the event of an emergency. In our experience, the best way to complete one is to start by asking the parent to complete as much as possible. Staff from your medical AP may begin this process, but it must be completed and owned by you, the learner's home school. Specific information about which members of staff a learner will meet with, locations in the school where medications are stored, and details about participation in sports or other practical subjects can only be added by a member of your staff.

Next, you should consult with relevant medical practitioners to check and amend the plan. Your school health nurse may do this or function as a bridge between you and a consultant or other specialist. If there is a need to administer medication or perform some other medical intervention, school staff may need specific training to support the learner (see Chapter 12). Your learner may be supported by a team of specialist nurses, and they will be a reliable source of advice and training. This is particularly the case for conditions such as diabetes, cancer, and asthma for example.

Finally, the document should be shared with all those in school who need to understand its contents in order to support the child.

Although the IHCP will contain information about risk, such as what an emergency looks like and how to respond, it may also be necessary to create a risk assessment for the learner.

Effective communication is key

Parents know their child best, and effective communication with parents is crucial. Parents should have a full role in developing an IHCP and input into the reintegration plan and risk assessment. Parents will be involved at the sharp end of implementing any reintegration plan. They will be there to encourage their child out of bed, into their school uniform, and will often be transporting them to your school gates. You must have them on board and in agreement with the plan. Be aware however, that often parents need to be reassured that their child can achieve that which they may currently think is impossible, with the appropriate support.

Clear communication is essential through the phases of the reintegration process, including ongoing support once the learner is back in your school. Initially, the learner may be attending both settings, and if changes to times or lessons are not shared with them, their parents, and teachers supporting them, then the learner may find themselves in an anxiety-provoking situation which can result either in a setback or may even mean a temporary pause is needed. You may then need to allow time for further work to be completed with the learner to enable them to trust you in the process and achieve the desired outcome.

Self-reflection

- Do you use IHCP for learners who are reintegrating back to your school?
- How are you capturing the voice of the learner?
- How effective are your communications with parents and other multi-agency colleagues?

Identifying key adults in school

Within your school, the identification of key trusted adults is essential to aid and support the learner back into school. We would recommend that several of your staff are involved with clearly defined roles and responsibilities, particularly in large schools where communication may be more challenging. It is important not only to consider the learner's journey through the academic curriculum, but also the unstructured times and movement around the school. Returning to busy corridors and noisy break times can provoke worries and fears for the learner.

Throughout the initial stages of the process, the learner will require support from both AP staff and your staff. Carefully planning reintegration will give the learner the best possible chance of success, but be prepared to be flexible as the learner is encountering complex thoughts and feelings during this time and there will be bumps in the road.

 **Case studies**

Shiva's story

Shiva has a complex medical condition with associated acute anxiety and was out of school for one year. To begin the process, Shiva's CAMHS worker was informed that she would begin a gradual reintegration this term. The discussion focused on how best we and CAMHS could work in partnership to support her throughout the period of transition.

Shiva began 1–1 sessions twice a week with a member of AP staff to support reintegration. They began by completing 'wishes and feelings' to listen to her voice around the reintegration back to their home school.

Shiva and her parent met with the key worker from her school at the medical AP. The medical AP lead for reintegration also sat in the meeting to aid discussion and support Shiva sharing any concerns she had. Shiva was worried about unsupervised time and what to say if one of her classmates asked why she had not been in school. The reintegration leader reassured

Shiva that the timetable would be written with her and that CAMHS and all teachers would be working in partnership to support her, particularly around anxiety-provoking social interactions.

Shiva and her mum visited school reception to meet the keyworker on the school site. Following the visit, Shiva returned to the AP and reluctantly chose which lesson she wanted to take part in first. Shiva expressed concerns about the return to her home school, so an additional week of support was added in.

The first lesson Shiva attended at school was supported by a reintegration HLTA from the AP. Shiva then returned to the AP setting for all other lessons throughout the week. Towards the end of the week, Shiva chose another lesson to attend with the support of the AP HLTA.

The following week the same two lessons were attended, with a review meeting planned at the end of the week with Shiva and her parents, school, and CAMHS where the next increase to time in school was agreed. Shiva wanted to extend her time to include a full morning at school. The reintegration HLTA supported Shiva in the new lessons, and she wanted to be in the other lessons unsupported. The increase was for two weeks, with Shiva not attending her AP setting in the afternoons of the morning visits to school.

Shiva then built her time to add on another lesson on a different day of the week. New lessons were supported by the alternative provisions HLTA, and no new lessons added for two weeks.

The following increase was for Shiva to stay at lunchtime. The school provided a small inclusion room where she could eat lunch with a couple of friends. This agreement was for two weeks.

The next review was held at school. The focus was now very much on Shiva building her time at school attending either mornings or afternoons, as Shiva no longer attended the AP. School introduced key members of staff to support her, and the AP offered daily support for new lessons for an hour a day.

Once Shiva was accessing her home school for more than 50% of the time a final review was called at school, where the AP ceased working with her.

Niall's story

Niall is a 15-year-old boy diagnosed with bone cancer. He spent a prolonged period in hospital undergoing cancer treatment and bone reconstruction. The teachers based in the hospital school liaised with his home school staff to maintain a level of education that he could comfortably manage while undergoing treatment. A key member of staff in the home school was identified as the point of contact. In this case, the head of year fulfilled this role.

After some months, a telepresence robot was introduced so Niall could participate in key school lessons from his hospital bed. This was organised by the hospital school in close consultation with Niall's home school.

Following hospital treatment, Niall was discharged home but was advised by doctors not to return to school for a period of six weeks as he was neutropenic, i.e. his immune system was weakened making him more prone to infection. Teaching was delivered in the home by the hospital school outreach team alongside the continued use of the telepresence robot in selected lessons.

A gradual reintroduction to school was planned by the hospital school staff alongside Niall, his family, and his head of year.

Niall was making steady progress over a number of weeks, so it was agreed that his school would take over the plan without further medical AP involvement. An agreement was reached for the medical AP to check in by telephone with the school at 2, 6, and 12 weeks.

Niall was highly motivated to maintain his academic studies, and social interaction was continued with friends visiting the home and via online contact, in particular video gaming. A very inclusive approach was adopted from his school headteacher, and throughout the school leadership team, ensuring that all staff engaged with the robot and the reintegration plan throughout.

Courtney's story

Courtney was admitted to a Child and Adolescent Mental Health Services (CAMHS) inpatient unit with an eating disorder. With the permission of her parents, the medical AP team within the unit contacted her school as soon as she was admitted. The school provided assessment and progress data, schemes of work, and access to an online learning platform. This assisted the medical AP staff in helping Courtney stay up to date with her learning during admission.

A key member of school staff was identified and invited to the Care Programme Approach (CPA) meetings that take place every four weeks. Permission was sought from Courtney and her parents about how much the school should be involved in discussions around her mental health difficulties and treatment. The staff member from school was invited into part of the CPA meetings. It was expected from the outset that the Courtney would return to her school once her treatment was complete.

The medical AP liaised with the school to understand specific problems Courtney had experienced with bullying at school with the aim of ensuring these issues were resolved before she returned. Information about incidents at school were fed back to the medical team who incorporated this into their psychology sessions with Courtney. Staff from the medical AP worked with Courtney to plan what she was going to say to her peers about where she had been while she was absent from school.

During Courtney's stay in the unit, the medical team constantly reviewed her progress towards recovery and eventually a discharge date was set. At this point, the CPA meetings became Discharge Planning Meetings. The school received support from the community eating disorders team about how to manage mealtimes at school for Courtney. Once the medical team assessed she was ready, Courtney was accompanied to school by staff from the medical AP. Initially this was for one Art lesson, but the length of time and the number of lessons increased over the next three visits.

When Courtney was finally discharged from the unit, she had a phased return to school over a period of three weeks. The medical AP offered support for two weeks following discharge.

School is the best place for learning!

The end goal is to reintegrate a learner back to their home school as their school environment is the best place to widen access to subjects, build resilience, and prepare for their next stages in education or training.

Once the reintegration is fully complete and the learner is accessing education in your school, ongoing support via a 'plan, do, review cycle' is advised. Should the learner hit a bump in the road then the medical AP can offer consultation and support to your staff to help the learner remain in your school.

The reintegration process is very delicate, and each step needs to be carefully planned and implemented. An anxious learner arriving at school and not being greeted by the expected member of staff can set back the reintegration by weeks or stop it in its tracks. Use a reintegration profile to record key events in the reintegration process so that everyone involved can keep up to date with events and changes.

Self-reflection

Ask yourself these questions:

- Is there an attitude of welcoming all learners transmitted by the staff in your school? If not, what can you do to change it?
- What has happened to the learner to bring them to this point?
- Which subjects or teachers are they going to find it easier to re-engage with?
- Are there particular times of the day that are difficult? Often the unstructured times such as before and after school, breaks, and lunchtimes are the most difficult for learners with anxiety difficulties.
- Are there concerns about access to toilets?
- Does the child need to take medication, eat, or drink outside of break and lunchtime?

You can see easy solutions to these problems, but in the mind of the learner they may represent an insurmountable barrier, so it is worth thinking them through before any planning meetings.

5 top tips

1. Start with an inclusive outlook – make it clear that you want the learner back and are open to making reasonable adjustments to make this happen.
2. Ensure clarity of aims and objectives, agreed by all parties.
3. Break the long-term goal into smaller steps then break these down further into achievable baby steps. Plan with, not to, the learner and their family.
4. Create a time-bound plan whilst acknowledging that timescales may change depending on the presentation of the learner. Acknowledge that reintegration is not linear; there will be ups and downs and some relapse is inevitable.
5. Continue support beyond the return to school.

SECTION 3

Working with hospital settings

14 Supporting learners in paediatric hospitals

Jayne Franklin

Introduction

As you have already picked up this book to read, we can assume that perhaps you are more likely to have had experience of a learner being admitted for a long stay in hospital. However, it is fair to say that thousands of teachers across the country may never actually have had this experience in their classroom, and so we hope that this next chapter gives some insight into what can be the most isolating and challenging of times for children and young people during their school career.

During a hospital admission, learners often have things done to or for them, resulting in reduced control over their environment and activities. Despite these challenges, teachers within inpatient paediatric settings take every opportunity to engage patients in their learning, whether recurrent, long stay, or even palliative. Through the inspiration and guidance of skilled teachers and support staff, learners can try things out, succeed and fail, but crucially lead and take control at their own pace.

What might a school within a paediatric hospital setting look like?

Inpatient education for learners may take place in a variety of medical settings but most commonly in tertiary referral paediatric-only centres. These are clinical settings which only accept patients referred by other consultants from other hospitals. The learners admitted into these paediatric hospitals,

DOI: 10.4324/9781003478942-17

wards, and units often have a range of severe medical and/or psychological conditions and hence special needs, although not always in the normally accepted educational sense.

What is more familiar and relatable to children than school of course?

School is a place where learners and their families attend for 190 days each year from the age of 5 to at least 16, and other than their own homes, school provides a relatable and consistent environment through some of the most influential periods of their lives.

Of course, when you visit a large children's hospital or a CAMHS inpatient unit, your traditional vision of a school and the environment you and your learners may be used to may not be completely realised. It is important to recognise the variety and diverse nature of teaching available in these medical settings in order to understand the experience of the learner in your classroom.

- We don't always work in a 'classroom'.
- We don't always have access to a private teaching space.
- We often teach at the bedside or open plan bays.
- Attendance at our school can't be compulsory.
- We do not always know who we are teaching on any given day.
- There are no consistent cohorts or groups.
- All ability levels, special needs, and ages are welcome.
- We may work as a 'host centre' to ensure young people can sit examinations even when in hospital at short notice.
- A parent, carer, or nurse may be part of the lesson.
- Remote learning will add value to their learning.
- **We are in a sense 'a school without walls'.**

Despite the huge limitations this may conjure in your minds, it allows for a highly personalised curriculum, with carefully planned, relevant, creative activities that present the perfect antidote to a tough clinical environment and inspire a continuity and love of learning.

So, how might you see school being delivered to an inpatient?

Each learner who is admitted to hospital for a period of time will of course experience this differently, depending where in the country they are and the availability of teaching and how settings are funded through the local authority or through an academy.

What is important to you as a teacher is to find a key contact and build your own picture from there. It might be as straightforward as finding the website for the school within the hospital's webpage, or you may need to identify the policy or named person responsible for the education of learners who are unable to attend school due to medical needs in the local authority (see Chapter 4).

What should be consistent for long-stay admissions is the provision of teaching which enables patients to continue their development as normally as possible, enhancing their learning, alleviating their anxiety about their schoolwork, as well as helping them and their families to cope with their treatment.

Best practice would be that school and prior education are raised as part of the clinical admissions process and information shared with clinicians is then recorded on electronic patient records. This means the clinical teams have some information about previous attendance at school and any additional learning needs. The education team in the hospital (usually a hospital school or medical AP) would engage with the patient and their family to gather additional information, before liaising with their home school to support assessing needs and planning educational input.

Most learners taught as inpatients remain the responsibility of the home school and should be recorded on their home school's annual census return. A hospital school will still collect their own data on attendance, assessment, achievement, and communications solely related to school and not the NHS.

Teaching is delivered to patients where their health permits as:

- a daily one-to-one lesson on the ward by the bedside
- a group session on the ward in a dedicated side room or space
- morning or afternoon sessions in a dedicated schoolroom space

- a mentoring and tutoring session using approved and quality assured providers
- a virtual session with teaching staff.

The strong relationships between teachers and learners, alongside a truly creative and wide variety of engaging approaches, unites groups of children who have never met, creating a unique sense of belonging and inclusion, even amongst strangers. This is a real boost to well-being and helps contribute to recovery.

Learning in an inpatient environment often needs a completely personalised approach for all learners including those with PMLD (Profound and Multiple Learning Difficulties). Teachers are dedicated to providing individualised support and guidance and a curriculum tailored to meet the needs of each learner. This personalised approach as described on Oxfordshire Hospital School's website, *'is a golden thread that is woven into the fabric'* of so many of these settings. Staff will often specialise in national curriculum subjects and deliver lessons across the age range and key stages, offering access to a range of external accreditation. Wherever possible, there are teachers who specialise in early years, primary, and core secondary subjects who can be deployed to work with the learners who need their expertise.

Hospital schools are constantly looking for new ways of inspiring learning and regularly invite writers, scientists, storytellers, local museums, artists, and musicians to share their passion with their learners, often incorporating workshops with celebrating special events like World Book Day. Many learners may find themselves in hospital for weeks, or confined to their home, and so this sense of normality is vital to how education is delivered.

Self-reflection

- Have you had the experience of one of your learners going into hospital for a period of treatment?
- Did you know that there were education teams in hospitals to support learners during their treatment?
- What do you think some of the challenges of delivering education in this environment might be?

Collaborative learning and working together – expectations and strategies

Continuity of education is vital for learners to enable them to reach their life goals and to fulfil their potential. A learner during a period of medical isolation at UCLH asked *'How can you expect me to become a doctor if you don't allow me to go to the schoolrooms?'* – an honest reflection that all partners had to consider long and hard in terms of accessibility to learning and the difficulty of infection control policies. But if we can push ourselves professionally and consider the starting points and needs of learners and their families, thrust into an often-frightening new environment, the difference is tangible. One learner at Great Ormond Street Hospital in a slogan competition, when asked to describe his experience of school during a long admission in hospital wrote, *'School in hospital was the best of times at the worst time'.*

Inpatient education in hospital schools never loses sight of the fact that if a learner does not have a positive experience of learning whilst they are an inpatient, they can lose interest, motivation, and potentially fall behind in their schoolwork. This means that a successful reintegration back to their school once they are recovered can be hard to achieve.

This means it is crucial that as teaching professionals we take any and every opportunity to engage inpatients and to collaborate with their home schools to ensure continued achievement and engagement. It is also essential that professionals are prepared to work collaboratively to create innovative school spaces which facilitate continuing education and social contact with peers acknowledging the positive impact these have on helping patients overcome their medical condition (LeHo Project, 2016).

The 'Review of educational provision for children unable to attend school for medical reasons' (Mintz, Palaiologoi, and Carroll, 2018) identified the significant impact collaboration across teams can have on a learner's progress whilst they are in hospital. This may seem obvious or even insulting to include here but is worth mentioning as it should never be taken for granted. This study notes that effective collaboration involves:

- a clear understanding of each other's role
- mutual respect
- value for what each stakeholder can offer to the holistic treatment of patients.

So how can this be achieved when a learner may possibly be miles away from their classroom, in a large paediatric hospital, in a small, isolated side room, and how can school leaders support this?

Be aware of what is happening outside the classroom

Leadership at all levels can empower teachers and support staff to be brave and to develop relationships both within and outside of their classroom settings that help ultimately to facilitate learning wherever learners may be. Teachers can very easily become isolated in their approaches to teaching and learning, but inward-looking practice would be a disservice to a community of learners with medical needs who overcome incredible adversity every day and who have a thirst for learning, keen to re-engage with the world when they are healthy enough to.

Self-reflection

- Take a moment to explore the website of the hospital that your learner is in – understand the setting they are now in and how their locality may have changed. Is there a local context or history that could be explored or taken advantage of whist an inpatient? If you know which ward they have been admitted to? Try to understand the staffing structure on the wards and who may be the best point of contact outside of the teachers and hospital school provision.
- Consider what learning opportunities there may be for them whilst in hospital – could you offer ideas that veer away from your standard curriculum? E.g. GCSE Biology assignment on germs where the learner could get advice from health professionals working in the hospital.

Start from the learner and their family

Parents and carers are often thrust suddenly into multiple roles when their child is admitted to hospital, moving from being 'simply a parent' to companion, nurse, tutor, caregiver, and confidant and this can be truly overwhelming. Parents have often told us that 'school' is the last thing on their minds as they navigate their new environment which in hindsight is completely understandable.

As a school, take time to call them and listen, drop them a regular email, or leave a personal voice message which tells them you have not forgotten about them or their child. Try to hear what they need in that moment, rather than imposing what you may need or require as a school at this stage. This is hugely influential on their continuing connection with you.

Self-reflection

- Who in your school has the best relationship with the family? It is essential that trust and respect are prioritised and are now more important than ever, and that the family are not overwhelmed by messages.
- Don't be afraid to ask about the treatment plan they are about to undertake, and reassure them that you will do all you can to build links with the relevant teams within the hospital.
- In addition to the teaching team, making a contact on the ward, a play worker, or a clinical nurse specialist can be helpful at this stage so as not to over-rely on the family.

A parent or carer may offer you the opportunity to talk directly to the learner themselves, and as we know children are the best advocates for their own needs and will soon share honestly about how you might best support them whilst in hospital. The child's own voice is essential and unique so please find as many ways as you can to capture this.

Sharing

Whether early years, adolescent, or in-between, we find that our learners respond to school sessions with curiosity, imagination, and enthusiasm which is no mean feat when you consider their unique starting points medically, emotionally, and academically. This can only happen when teachers are enabled to engage critically with other professional settings, share resources, and have the space to develop their skills and interests.

This can be as simple as sharing lesson plans or curriculum maps with the hospital teachers, but without wanting to patronise any professionals, here are some additional examples of sharing that experience tells us can make a significant impact:

- Shared assessments and marking, e.g. a piece of work completed in hospital that is marked by both the hospital and home school then discussed with the learner.
- Use of technology to remotely join lessons or assemblies (see also Chapter 9).
- Opportunities for patients to share their learning achievements whilst in hospital with their school – could they have an award, or their work be included in a display? This can really boost mood, morale, and the feeling of belonging.
- Weekly email contact from peers and/or teachers sharing news from school, or links to current work on virtual school platforms.
- Regular video messages from their peers organised by home schoolteachers.

Self-reflection

- Have you shared EHCPs, current learning goals, previous reports, learning strategies, and developmental needs of the patient with the teachers at the hospital? Your expertise and knowledge of the learner is crucial and will be needed by other professionals who will take this into account when developing their relationship with the learner in this new learning environment.

- Are you experiencing the same level of 'sharing' from the hospital school team?
- It can be helpful to agree expectations of each other when the learner is admitted so sharing is as effective as possible.

Visits

Schools are without a doubt under the most significant pressure during the current economic post-pandemic climate that they have ever been. Budgets are tight and the day-to-day pressures of simply keeping school communities on an even keel are not to be underestimated. But we are here to offer strategies and advice to our often-invisible community of learners who are long-stay inpatients in hospital.

If you can find a way with your school leaders to enable a pre-arranged visit, even if it involves a long train journey out of your area, experience shows how empowering this can be for all involved. Sharing and learning new skills alongside other professionals not only offers a different insight to staff CPD but demonstrates to the learner the seriousness with which professionals take working together to ensure progress can continue. In some cases, hospital schools may even be able to offer financial support to reimburse travel expenses to facilitate the visit, and we would encourage making that enquiry.

If you can visit, the hospital school team will prepare you for the nature of the ward, any infection control precautions you need to take, and will guide you sensitively, based on the needs of the patient. Although hospital teachers are used to working in these circumstances, they appreciate how challenging this can be for visitors.

 **Case study**

Rowan's story

When we first met Rowan, he was very much at the start of processing the trauma of developing a sudden health need. His mental health deteriorated further when the reality of having to be on dialysis became apparent. He had just started to overcome this when he experienced sudden, profound hearing loss which further impacted on all parts of his life.

Rowan's relationship with the hospital school team developed quickly as he grew more confident knowing the routines of the hospital and the school. He was able to tell us if he was not feeling well and was better placed to accept help more readily. Rowan found the intensity of the one-to-one sessions with a teacher in hospital quite difficult, and he presented as quiet and introverted, but over time, with input from a familiar and consistent teacher, this began to change.

Rowan's confidence in his ability in English increased significantly when he saw the link between his work in the hospital and what his peers were doing at school. This positively impacted on his mood, and he became more engaged in his learning in both settings. Every week, Rowan asked to take his book home from hospital to show what learning he had completed whilst in hospital.

On regular dialysis, Rowan made a positive relationship with another primary aged dialysis patient and when this patient was discharged, it highlighted the importance of continuing social interaction with peers. The two are still in contact.

Rowan has now engaged with a hospital play worker for the first time on the ward, and has enjoyed engaging in other activities, including chef's sessions and participating in the end-of-term collaborative film production, all of which has been very positive for him.

Both his mood and his enthusiasm for learning have improved since he can return to his school between hospital admissions. Rowan's home school has gone to great lengths to facilitate this, which has not only given his family more confidence in the school, but also enabled Rowan more time to access learning and be with his peers.

Transitioning home

Supporting the transition of a learner from a hospital school back to their home school, or perhaps a new environment, requires careful planning and collaboration to ensure a smooth and supportive reintegration. Here are some key steps to facilitate this transition that follow on from earlier strategies mentioned in this chapter:

- Planning and Communication – as already emphasised, regular communication between the hospital school, the home school, parents, and healthcare providers is crucial. Set up a meeting involving all relevant parties to discuss the learner's needs, progress, and any necessary adjustments or accommodations. Remember there may be new strategies needed to support changing medical, emotional, and educational needs. Consider involving the learner in the planning process to ensure their preferences and concerns are addressed.

- Educational Support and Adjustments – many hospital schools often provide detailed reports that can guide current assessments of the learner's academic progress and identify any gaps or areas needing extra support. Implementing necessary adjustments, such as a phased return to school, modified timetables, or additional support from teaching assistants or tutors will be important to consider and discuss with the family. Engage external agencies such as educational psychologists, social workers, or specialised support organisations if additional expertise or resources are needed and ask the hospital school for additional evidence as needed to help any referrals you need to make.

- Emotional and Social Support (see also Chapter 7) – often the clinical teams in the hospital will have links with relevant charities or local organisations who may be able to provide emotional support through counselling services, peer mentoring programs, or support groups. Do ask the patient experience or PALs teams within hospital for advice – do not think the school need to have all the answers as every condition is different and there are specialist teams who can help. Encourage peer support by assigning a buddy or mentor to help the learner navigate the pressures of returning to the school social environment and reintegrate into the school community.

- Healthcare Coordination – the family will often have the best contacts to help the school coordinate with healthcare providers to ensure any ongoing medical needs are met. Clinical Nurse Specialists are your best friends in this situation and can help train school staff on any specific medical conditions or emergency procedures relevant to the learner as needed.

By following these steps, you can create a supportive environment that helps the learner transition smoothly from a hospital school back to their next steps in education, addressing both their academic and emotional needs.

5 top tips

1. Keep the learner in mind and include them in discussions at school so they do not become invisible.
2. Maintain regular email contact with teachers in the hospital and visit if you can.
3. Provide time for meetings or short conversations to address any emerging family concerns promptly.
4. Be flexible and ready to adjust plans based on feedback from teachers, parents, and the learner themselves.
5. Regularly update learners on what is happening in their home community – help them to remain connected and maintain a sense of belonging.

References

Mintz, J. Palaiologoi, I. & Carroll, C. (2018). *A review of educational provision for children unable to attend school for medical reasons.* University College London, Institute of Education. Accessed at https://www.researchgate.net/publication/339055573_A_review_of_educational_provision_for_children_unable_to_attend_school_for_medical_reasons on 20.09.2024.

Oxfordshire Hospital School website https://ohs.oxon.sch.uk/ accessed 20.09.2024.

The LeHo Hospital Project (2016) accessed at https://www.lehoproject.eu/en/#:~:text=The%20LeHo%20WEBINARS%20are%20meant,place%20between%20May%20%E2%80%93%20December%202016 on 20.09.2024.

15

Supporting learners in Child and Adolescent Mental Health units

Karen Ingham and Lorraine Coady

Introduction

The experience of becoming an inpatient in a Child and Adolescent Mental Health Services (CAMHS) unit is an extremely uncertain time for a learner and their family. The educational provision in a CAMHS unit is essential in supporting the mental health and educational needs of that learner, alongside the clinical team. The actions of your school during the admission can be beneficial to a learner's recovery, but negative practices can lead to feelings of rejection and hopelessness, making it harder for them to return when they are discharged from the unit.

The purpose of this chapter is to provide a guide for your school to help you understand how you can best support academic progress and emotional well-being during a hospital admission. It will provide learner views of what actions by your school are helpful and cover the following areas:

- What happens in a CAMHS unit
- Communication and collaboration
- Maintaining educational continuity
- Preparing for discharge and reintegration
- Signposting of resources that schools might find useful.

DOI: 10.4324/9781003478942-18

By adopting these best practices, you can help ensure that learners not only recover from their mental health challenges but thrive and avoid readmission to hospital.

What happens in a CAMHS unit

CAMHS inpatient units are dedicated to the assessment and treatment of children and adolescents experiencing severe mental health issues. These issues can involve suicidal ideation, significant self-harm, eating disorders, and episodes of psychosis. The units often have extensive multidisciplinary teams which can include psychiatrists, psychologists, nurses, therapists, education staff, and social workers. The team work towards the common goal of stabilising the learner's mental health, developing a treatment plan, and supporting transition back to the community, which will include a return to school or college.

CAMHS units differ from other wards in that the length of admission is often unknown. In medical wards treatment plans often have an estimated length of time. However, due to the complexity in treating mental health conditions, it is often difficult to predict when a discharge will occur. This can be very unsettling for a learner.

The first few days after admission can be a busy time and may not be the best time for you to check in with a learner or their family. On admission to the ward, a learner will undergo various assessments and be seen by numerous health staff. They will also have to adjust to being in hospital away from their families and with other adolescents on a ward.

CAMHS units will normally hold an admissions meeting which you may be invited to attend. If you become aware that one of your learners has been admitted to a CAMHS hospital, the best first point of contact is the CAMHS hospital school team. They can provide advice on how the admissions process works and when it is appropriate to make contact.

During an admission, there will be set meeting points where professionals come together with the learner to discuss treatment and set goals for recovery. If the learner agrees, it is good practice for you, as their home school, to attend these so you can be involved in planning for reintegration to the community. However, as sensitive health information is being discussed, the learner, or parent or carer, will need to give permission for this to happen.

Where a learner has the capacity to make decisions, they will make the decision whether you or another representative from the school can visit.

Communication and collaboration

Learners on a CAMHS unit have varying needs when managing risk. The significant risk means that some items may be considered unsafe to bring onto a unit. If you visit the unit, you should check the requirements. Medium secure units may require items such as mobile phones to be left in lockers. Some units may require bag checks. Items that might be considered negligible risk in the community could cause harm and you may be asked not to bring such things on to the unit. Visiting hours vary from unit to unit but many offer flexibility in visiting times.

It can be challenging to decide how much or how little contact is helpful. The CAMHS unit hospital school can play a role in finding the right level of contact. It is important to prioritise the needs of the learner above your needs as a school. You will understandably want to do your best for the learner but might not have a full picture of the treatment. Too much contact or too little contact may be unhelpful, and needs will vary from case to case.

CAMHS unit hospital schools will usually phone you to liaise with you on the admission. Many will send a liaison form to you to complete. One of the issues that CAMHS hospital teams face is that these forms might take time to be returned. Receiving the form promptly means that a learner can have continuity during what is already an unsettling time. Learners we speak to say that when the CAMHS hospital school knows about the courses they are on, and things they need help with, it tells them that you, their home school, are thinking about them and care about them.

The CAMHS meeting structure has already been mentioned. Being seen at these meetings by a learner provides them with a connection to the structure and routine that was in place before they became unwell.

Collaboration with a learner is also important. Arranging for a trusted staff member or yourself to visit is often welcome. However, the CAMHS hospital school will know the best point for this to happen.

Some learners are too unwell to continue with their usual range of school subjects, or to attend the CAMHS hospital school full time. The timely action of you and other staff in the school is important in providing enough information for the education team to act on. It is also important to realise that having the same expectations around schoolwork of a learner who is a CAMHS inpatient may be unrealistic.

Self-reflection

- Do you complete liaison paperwork in a timely manner, acknowledging that learners want to know that they are doing the right sort of work and that it will help them when they return?
- Do you include vital information about ability and courses?
- Can you familiarise yourself with the admissions process, find out what meetings will occur, and ask if you can be part of these?

Preparing for discharge and reintegration

In the run-up to discharge from hospital, learners may have extended periods of 'leave'. This may involve overnight stays in the family home. The priority at this time is to learn how to stay safe in a community environment. Attending their home school may be part of this process. If you attend the discharge planning meeting, where possible, it will give you the best ideas of how this can be managed.

As part of the preparation for discharge, it may also be necessary to understand the 'safety plan' for a learner. This type of plan will outline any potential triggers that might result in risk and how any presenting risks can be managed. You will need to support a learner to manage their plan. Discharge is an incredibly stressful time for a learner and taking their wishes into account about communicating their return and how they will be reintegrated into the school is essential.

The risk of relapse with mental health conditions is real schools, as well as community services, play a significant role in reducing this risk. When schools engage in the planning process there is a greater chance of successful reintegration.

What young people say

Discussions with young people both during and after admission bring up the same common themes around being held in mind by their home schools and colleges.

'I want to be remembered by my school'.
Learners often know what friends and classmates are doing both in school and out of school. In many types of CAMHS units they have access to mobile phones and social media, and they often feel that life is going on without them. There are a number of things that you can do to help them feel included, e.g. you could make use of AVI robots, where the robot is in the learner's seat and the learner can join the lesson virtually (see Chapter 10). Whilst this option is not available or appropriate for everyone, learners who have used the robots say it has helped them feel included. CAMHS hospital schools have qualified teachers who can support with learning, but they will need access to the online tasks and passwords to prepare to support learners with their learning.

Many learners welcome contact from you, their home school. They say it is important that the 'right person' comes to see them on the unit, and this might be a form tutor, or a subject teacher, and will depend on who has a relationship with the learner. Virtual catch-ups can be scheduled regularly, or ad hoc. The CAMHS hospital schools can support in setting these up.

'I want to carry on with my "real work" from school'.
Some schools are excellent at providing work that is beyond a worksheet. They can send curriculum plans and resources. However, a learner having their actual exercise books and the log-in to the virtual learning platform can be a game changer. The qualified teachers on the unit can help prioritise the workload if they can see what peers in the learner's home school are learning. This has additional benefits, such as the learner feeling connected to school, and being 'held in mind'. Any work they do in hospital can more easily be felt to be relevant and meaningful, which is important when they begin to return to school.

'I want to be invited to my prom'.

This is both about being remembered as part of the year group and having the same opportunity to complete year 11 in the same way as their peers. It also is about being accepted and wanting to visit. We all know that leaving school, e.g. at the end of a year, a key stage, or when you have finished statutory schooling, is a rite of passage for a learner.

Some home schools have supported learners well at key transition points. For example, one school made a real effort to ensure a learner was included in a yearbook. Everyone wants their shirt to be signed at the end of year 11.

Self-reflection

• How can you facilitate inclusion for these learners at key transitions?

Home schools are sometimes nervous about having a learner with significant risk of self-harm at a school prom. However, CAMHS school and hospital staff can support with the development of a safety plan and may be able to provide escort staff if it is deemed appropriate by the hospital and the school.

'I want to sit my GCSEs' or 'I don't want to sit my GCSEs this year, I can't manage it all'.

Some students have been really upset that their home school has decided to withdraw them from exams. This is even the case where both at the home and CAMHS hospital school, the learner could not cope with all the exams. How this information is communicated to the learner, so they have ownership of the decision, is important. It is also important to note that recovery from some conditions, such as psychosis, can be very sudden. We have had learners in our settings achieve better grades than home schools originally predicted after recovering and having intensive tuition whilst in hospital.

Exemptions can be applied for some components of courses if learners are unable to complete them. For example, science requiring practical investigations cannot be completed on a medium secure unit if the risk is too high. A home school can also apply for special consideration if a learner has been absent for an exam or has sat the exam, but the school believes they have been disadvantaged. Examples of this that might be observed in a CAMHS setting are stress, anxiety, or panic attack on the day of the exam. The awarding body decides on special consideration and how much a percentage (up to 5%) they may award or in the case of an absent candidate, take an average of the other papers sat for the same course.

Home schools or hospital schools can put access arrangements in place through the school SENCO. Examples of this could be rest breaks, coloured paper, or white noise during exams. Emergency access arrangements can also be put in place by the CAMHS hospital school. It is essential that home schools liaise closely with the exams officer and SENCO to ensure learners get the right access and consideration during exams. When a learner comes to a hospital school but has already been entered by their home school, we will liaise with them to arrange a 'transfer candidate' application. This is to put arrangements in place to allow the candidate to sit the exams at the hospital.

'What has the school told the other teachers, and my friends? I need to know what people know about me'.

Some learners feel so ashamed and anxious about the stigma attached to being in a psychiatric hospital that they invent a cover story for their admission. This could be travelling abroad, starting a different school, or having a physical illness. Some choose to break all virtual contact with friends from their former school, unsure how to answer questions about their sudden absence. Home school staff need to plan how best to support a young person with this.

'My school said they have taken me off roll, they say it's in my best interests, because of my mental health needs'.

Schools are not permitted to just off roll a learner, and off rolling is not in the best interests of the learner. Many professionals working in hospital schools have seen off rolling happen and the impact this has on a learner. The words of one learner describes the sense of shock they felt when their school took them off roll:

'I really loved school, and I couldn't believe it when I was told I didn't go there anymore. I felt betrayed'.

'My school think I'm too risky to be able to go back. I shouldn't have said I still think about suicide, or self-harm'.

Many learners try to manage their own mental health needs in school by using self-harming behaviours, often unknown to their schools. Learners who will have had no contact with services who attend mainstream settings may unfortunately show self-harming behaviours.

What parents and carers say

There are two common concerns from parents and carers, and we often see polar expectations in different families. Some parents express concern about their child falling behind and others feel that their child should not have to deal with the pressure of schoolwork whilst in hospital. Home schools play an important part in managing the expectations of parents.

'Will they be able to keep up with their schoolwork?'

This is unlikely due to the number of therapies that the learner might need during an admission. They are at a point of crisis, and the priority of the admission must be treatment and recovery. Learning is part of this and provides important structure and routine. The education will need to focus on key aspects of the curriculum that the learners can manage at this point in their journey. Units and home schools will work together to prioritise this curriculum and aim to meet necessary deadlines. It is unreasonable to think the learner can do both full-time education and undertake psychiatric treatment.

'They shouldn't have to go to school, they aren't well'.

Structure and routine support recovery, and school is a normal part of everyday life. The CAMHS hospital school will be the most ordinary part of a learner's day. The intellectual endeavour of education can provide hope for the future and build aspiration. Learners who engage well with education often have a more successful reintegration into their home school.

'It was the first time in the school system where I felt heard, and that my success and aspirations mattered to the staff. Whilst previous discussions of my progress and trajectory were on reflection negative, by talking about reducing expectations and making "realistic plans", the hospital school staff made me feel that what I desired and wanted from life was achievable'.

You, the home school staff, can make an enormous difference to educational progress in hospital, recovery, and reduce the chance of relapse. However, there are several practices that are unhelpful. Consider the questions in the self-reflection to ascertain if you engage in unhelpful practices.

Self-reflection

- Do you take learners off roll whilst they are in hospital?
- Do you make decisions about qualifications that they will not manage to do without consultation with the CAMHS hospital school, the learner, and their parent?
- Do you make decisions about risk, making statements like 'They are too risky to have back on site', or 'We can't have pupils who self-harm here'?
- Do you have inflexible policies that do not allow learners to repeat the year? It would be helpful if consideration is given to such requests if it is in the best interest of the learner.
- Do you assume that controlled assessments cannot be completed in hospital?
- Do you assume that because there are often no science laboratories, and geography field trips may not be possible, there are no alternatives to completing coursework and assessments?
- Do you make plans for the learner without involving all stakeholders, e.g. planning to remove a student from roll, not entering for exams, changing GCSE options without consultation?

5 top tips

1. A CAMHS hospital school is an intervention, not a destination. Home schools need to be part of the admissions to discharge model and involve themselves in information sharing, collaboration, and multidisciplinary working.
2. Appoint a trusted adult whom your learner relates well to who will maintain contact with the learner during their admission.
3. Coproduction is the key to a successful hospital stay and discharge. Plans that are made without involving all stakeholders are less likely to be successful.
4. Technology, such as virtual learning environments, can be useful during a hospital admission.
5. Some learners sit exams when in hospital. Most CAMHS hospital schools have an exams officer and a SENCO who can advise on exams, access arrangements, and special considerations.

SECTION 4

Next steps

16

Children's health charities that can provide advice, support, and resources

Cath Kitchen, Daniella Rotimi
(Allergy UK), Tracey Dunn
(Anaphylaxis UK), Rajwant Kaur
Singh (Children's Heart Federation),
Sammie McFarland (Long Covid
Kids), Chelsea Wong (LUPUS UK),
Tina Coope (PANS PANDAS UK),
Catherine Hodder (Young Epilepsy),
Maria Marinho (Well at School), and
Michelle Allen (Versus Arthritis)

Introduction

The Health Conditions in Schools Alliance (http://healthconditionsinschools.org.uk) is a group of children's charities, all of whom provide support about their area of expertise in terms of medical conditions to children, young people, families, and other professionals in different ways. They collaborate, along with a wide variety of stakeholders including healthcare professionals and trade unions, to ensure learners with health conditions get the care and support they need to thrive in school. As a collective, representatives of these charities meet regularly and lobby the different political parties and policy makers to try to ensure that the voice of the learners they support and

DOI: 10.4324/9781003478942-20

their families are not forgotten or overlooked. Their website offers guidance and tools to schools who are looking after learners with health conditions. You can download a template medical conditions policy, a sample individual healthcare plan and advice on what it should contain, guidance on the legal situation across the UK, and a process for making sure learners who require education in different settings get the support they need.

These charities can be a valuable resource to support you in your practice. Below are extracts from some of the alliance members, and information about what support they can offer to you, to your staff, your learners, and their parents.

Links to all the resources can be found in the resources area, most of them are free of charge, are accredited and produced in collaboration with health professionals. Please make effective use of them!

Allergy UK

Allergy UK is the only charity to provide comprehensive assistance across the entire spectrum of allergies, ensuring no one faces these challenges alone. All manifestations of allergic disease are represented in the work we do. Our purpose extends to improving education around allergies among healthcare professionals, industry, and schools. We are steadfast in our mission to ensuring that allergies are taken seriously by everyone.

For schools, we offer comprehensive information covering policies and legislation, allergy action management plans, medication protocols, food allergies, school meal arrangements, 'no nut' policies, allergen restrictions, communication strategies, inclusivity and support initiatives, and addressing bullying concerns. All this information is accessible through the following link: https://www.allergyuk.org/living-with-an-allergy/at-school/for-schools/

Allergy UK top tips

- It is particularly important to establish well-defined and concise allergy policies that outline procedures for managing allergies on school premises.

- These policies should be effectively communicated to everyone involved in school settings, including staff, parents, learners, and caterers.
- Additionally, we recommend periodic reviews and updates to allergy policies and procedures each term, considering latest information, changes in learner needs, and best practices.

Anaphylaxis UK

Anaphylaxis UK has been supporting people living with serious allergies as a charity for 30 years, offering evidence-based information for individuals, their families, for businesses, and for schools and other places of education. Supported by the Clinical and Scientific Panel, we ensure that we have expert insight into health and scientific issues related to serious allergies, and associated research. We provide advice on current management of serious allergies so that we can support the allergic community. The panel currently consists of over 15 members including Professor Adam Fox, Professor Graham Roberts, and Dr Paul Turner, and our current Clinical and Scientific Panel chair is Dr Helen Evans-Howells, all of whom are exceptional in their field.

We have a long-established programme of support for schools and other educational settings including wrap around care and holidays clubs. Our Safer Schools programme has a wealth of information and resources which are free to download. The resources include guidance on good practice, a model policy which was written together with Allergy UK and British Society of Allergy and Clinical Immunology (BSACI) and is a one-stop shop for everything an educational establishment needs to be a safe and inclusive environment.

In addition to our leading course for schools, AllergyWise®, we have a range of courses that are suitable for all educational establishments. These are low-priced and come with access to further materials that enable schools to meet the requirements of the Relationships and Sex Education curriculum.

As there are 14 top food allergens that must be declared by law and with it being possible to be allergic to anything, food or non-food, we encourage schools to be inclusive in their practice by being allergy aware.

Anaphylaxis UK top tips

- Ensure you have an attitude of 'it could happen here' – this will keep learners safe.
- Check out guidance on the use of adrenaline auto-injectors in schools https://assets.publishing.service.gov.uk/media/5a829e 3940f0b6230269bcf4/Adrenaline_auto_injectors_in_schools.pdf

Children's Heart Federation

Heart conditions are the most common defect present at birth in the UK. Some 1 in 100 children are born with a congenital heart defect, 20–30% of whom will require surgery within the first year of life. Thousands more children will acquire a heart condition in infancy each year.

The Children's Heart Federation (CHF) is the leading national charity championing children with heart conditions. CHF is dedicated in empowering these children, their families, and carers.

Our vision is that all children with heart conditions have their medical and social needs met so they can live the fullest life possible. We collaborate with individuals and organisations to inform, inspire, and improve the lives of children with congenital and acquired heart disease.

Resources available on our website include information sheets detailing the specifics of many different heart conditions and how they might affect children; symptoms, treatment plans, and care pathways can be found here: https://chfed.org.uk/how-we-help/information-service/heart-conditions/

We also provide a suite of information sheets which focuses on lifestyle management for children with heart conditions: https://chfed.org.uk/how-we-help/information-service/caring-for-heart-children/

We have a section here dedicated to education, with information and guidance for anyone involved in the education of a child with a heart condition.

Children's Heart Federation top tips

- It is particularly important to identify the specific needs of a child with a heart condition.
- Collaboratively preparing appropriate plans with parents and the child's cardiac liaison nurse is vital.

Long Covid Kids

Long Covid Kids (LCK) is a leading charity dedicated to supporting families, children, and young people affected by Long Covid and related illnesses. Long Covid, also known as Post Covid Condition, involves symptoms persisting for three months or more after initial COVID-19. These symptoms can fluctuate in severity and affect any system in the body. Common symptoms in children include extreme fatigue, cognitive impairment, exercise intolerance (Post-Exertional Malaise, or PEM), and Postural Tachycardia Syndrome (PoTS), among many others.

The charity provides a range of support for families, children, and young people including support groups, resources, and signposting.

Resources and Support for Schools include a range of free resources to increase awareness and understanding of Long Covid among educators, ensuring they are equipped to support affected students, including the Educational Toolkit, Videos, and Handbook: https://www.longcovid-kids.org/educational-toolkit

Key topics include:

- Returning to Education: Guidelines on when and how children can appropriately return to school with Long Covid.
- Accessing and Engaging with Education: Strategies for reasonable adjustments to ensure inclusion and support, helping children reach their potential despite health challenges.

- Identifying Alternative Provisions: Information on available educational options and provisions to accommodate the needs of children with Long Covid if they are unable to attend school.
- Finding Additional Support: Guidance on making referrals, accessing extra support, and signposting to appropriate services.
- Understanding the Impact on the Family: Considering the family's perspective while managing a poorly understood condition, including issues of adjustment, overwhelm, and isolation.

In certain cases, LCK provides personalised support from a team of professionals, including an Occupational Therapist, an Educational Psychologist, and experts with lived experience of Long Covid. This individualised support addresses specific needs and challenges faced by children and young people with Long Covid.

By leveraging these resources, schools can support students with Long Covid, ensuring they have the best opportunity to succeed academically and thrive despite their health conditions.

Long Covid Kids top tips

- Early intervention and appropriate referral have a key role to play. Health may need to be prioritised for a prolonged period of time.
- Remember as one child said 'Just because I am in school, doesn't mean I am well'.

LUPUS UK

LUPUS UK is a charity that aims to raise awareness for the autoimmune condition lupus and provide support for the lupus community.

Lupus is an autoimmune condition where the immune system mistakenly identifies the body's own tissues as foreign invaders. The immune system produces too many antibodies which circulate through the bloodstream, consequently leading to inflammation in the body. Symptoms can include organ problems, fatigue, chronic pain, sun sensitivity, and more.

Lupus can be life-threatening and has no cure. However, with the right treatment, many live relatively normal lives. It can be especially difficult for children and young people to have the added challenges of this, as it can be isolating and overwhelming. It is important for schools to be aware of the impact of this condition and to provide the necessary support and accommodations so learners can excel.

Check out our information sheet for teachers: https://lupusuk.org.uk/wp-content/uploads/2024/08/LUPUS-Information-for-Teachers.pdf

LUPUS UK top tip

- Every individual living with lupus experiences it differently, so ensure to listen to what *they* have to say about their body and what they need. They know more than you think, and so listening to what they are going through, validating their experience, and producing a tailored plan is useful.

PANS PANDAS UK

PANS PANDAS UK is the only UK charity supporting children, young people, and their families living with the neuropsychiatric conditions Paediatric Acute-onset Neuropsychiatric Syndrome (PANS) and Paediatric Autoimmune Neuropsychiatric Disorders Associated with Streptococcal Infections (PANDAS).

We provide information and community support to children and families. We raise awareness of the symptoms and treatment options for healthcare professionals so that they are better equipped to recognise when a child may have PANS or PANDAS. We provide training in educational settings so that families and children living with these conditions receive the support they need to access appropriate education and thrive.

Following the recent recognition of these conditions by the NHS alongside significant health developments, an increasing number of schools are supporting learners with these diagnoses, and these numbers are only set to increase.

PANS PANDAS UK provides a wealth of education resources for families and professionals. Putting in early support can make a real difference to a child's educational outcomes. These resources can be accessed at https://www.panspandasuk.org/panspandas-for-educators

The charity has also been providing free and online CPD accredited training for a wide range of professionals including educational psychologists, specialist support teachers, SENCOs, and designated clinical officers amongst others. You can sign up on the website to access this training.

PANS PANDAS top tips

- Whilst the health situation is evolving, many families with a child with suspected PANS and PANDAS are still struggling to access a diagnosis and treatment. As support in school is based on needs (rather than diagnosis dependent) it is important to be aware that the needs in PANS and PANDAS can have both an abrupt and severe onset alongside a relapsing and remitting pattern.
- Schools can provide a crucial role in spotting the early signs and giving due attention to all the impacts. These can be wide-ranging and include cognitive, physical, social, emotional, and behavioural aspects.

Versus Arthritis

It is estimated that 10,000 children under 16 years old have been diagnosed with Juvenile Idiopathic Arthritis (JIA).

Versus Arthritis is the largest arthritis charity in the UK, and we have a dedicated 'Young People and Families' team that support young people in a clinic setting and provide holistic one-to-one support away from the hospitals. We also provide spaces for young people to build confidence and meet others who have similar conditions to build a peer support network. We do this by providing events, residentials, and workshops. We also provide support and resources to professionals, and you can contact us for any support.

Versus Arthritis has set up a 'School Project' to look at gaps in resources to support schools and young people and to break down the barriers they are facing. As part of the school project, we have already developed a series of 'short films' to be used on their own, as part of training, or with other resources, to raise awareness of the needs of young people with arthritis at school. Some of the films are for young people living with arthritis and their families, sharing top tips and support. Others are for school staff, highlighting how to create inclusive schools and support young people to thrive, and there is even a dedicated film for how to support young people to participate in PE. We have also delivered our first school webinar specifically for school staff to help support them to support their learners with arthritis.

We have produced a cross charity Individual Healthcare Plan for schools that supports young people with JIA and similar conditions and gives helpful hints and tips on what to cover in the plan to save you time.

Versus Arthritis top tip

- Do not be worried about including young people with JIA – use our resources to support you to help them thrive in your school.

Young Epilepsy

Young Epilepsy is the UK charity working with and for children and young people with epilepsy, standing up for their rights and ensuring their voices are heard.

Epilepsy is a neurological condition that disrupts the normal electrical activity our brains use to communicate with the rest of the body. This disruption causes repeated seizures. Seizures can take many forms because the brain is responsible for such a wide range of functions.

We want to ensure that children and young people with epilepsy are safe, included, and able to thrive at school. However, many of these children are not receiving the support and understanding to enable them to participate fully in school life. Young people and parents have shared their experiences of:

- Seizures missed or mistaken for not paying attention.
- School staff unaware of what to do when a seizure happens.
- Children unnecessarily excluded from learning, sports, and trips.

Young Epilepsy has free resources and training available to help those who work in schools create a safe and inclusive environment for all children and young people with epilepsy. These include a guide for schools on support-ing young people with epilepsy, including a template Individual Healthcare Plan, and class resources for children and young people.

Young Epilepsy top tips

- Epilepsy can affect everyone differently. Make sure the young per-son's Individual Healthcare Plan reflects their seizure type, their triggers, and the impact on their learning and well-being.
- Check out our website – www.youngepilepsy.org.uk.

Well at School

Although Well at School is not one of the charities, it is worthwhile high-lighting this as a useful source of information and guidance which is free of charge. Well at School (www.wellatschool.org), produced by Chelsea Community Hospital School, is an online resource helping schools support learners with medical and mental health conditions so they can fully engage in education. They work in partnership with health professionals, learners, and teachers to ensure content is relevant and up to date.

The aim of the site is to:

- Inform schools on a range of medical and mental health conditions affecting learners.

- Advise schools on how to enable learners to fully engage in school life.
- Promote awareness of the educational needs of learners living with medical and mental health conditions.
- Identify and promote relevant resources and policy guidance.

Well at School top tips

- The most up-to-date news, blogs, and articles are featured in the half-termly newsletter which can be sent directly to your inbox if you sign up via this form https://wellatschool.us2.list-manage. com/subscribe?u=f08adf337ac9aa8f384b9a50b&id=99371ad5a7
- You can also follow us on X for more regular updates @ wellatschool.

The Medical Needs in Schools project

Steve Lowe

Introduction

The Oxfordshire Hospital School (OHS) is an Oxfordshire County Council (OCC) maintained hospital school based across a number of settings throughout the county of Oxfordshire and is designated as a Special School. The school has three main settings where staff teach:

1. The Children's Hospital Teaching Sector that incorporates the Children's Hospital Oxford. This includes learners at Helen and Douglas House hospice, and inpatient learners at the Oxford Centre for Children and Young People in Pain.
2. Highfield Teaching Sector that incorporates the Highfield Unit, and the Meadow PICU, both Child and Adolescent Mental Health Units with the Meadow an intensive care unit.
3. Outreach Teaching Sector, for learners who are too unwell to go to school but who are not in hospital.

What is the Medical Needs in Schools project?

In 2017, Angela Ransby (the then headteacher at the OHS) met over coffee with Helen Griffiths, Consultant Psychologist with the Children's Paediatric Psychological Medicine Team at the Oxfordshire University Hospital (OUH). They ruminated on the challenges that schools experience when supporting their learners who have medical conditions and felt the

DOI: 10.4324/9781003478942-21

need to help. Already marginalised from society because of their ill health, this group of learners need more and need better; and so, a partnership between education and health was born in Oxford.

Aims of the project

The first stages of the project saw an invitation to schools to participate in a two-year pilot offering free training and support. The project's principal aim was to provide support for Oxfordshire schools in the management of medical needs within the education environment, in compliance with statutory and best practice guidance.

This would be achieved through:

- Training, consultation, and practical support for Oxfordshire schools on the statutory and best practice guidance.
- Improved links with, and knowledge of, local service pathways and resources.
- Developing and providing excellent clinical support pathways for learners with medical needs who are struggling with education in Oxfordshire through the hospital school, community paediatric medicine, and links with other appropriate services.
- Improvement of knowledge of the statutory and best practice guidance within wider networks who are stakeholders in supporting learners with medical needs – the acute hospitals, local mental health services, and local authority.
- Robustly evaluating and disseminating the learning from project activity, to inform educators, decision-, and policy-makers at a local and national level.

Year 1 of the project

During year 1, all Oxfordshire schools were invited to the launch and given the opportunity to sign up as a partnership school. Eighteen schools were confirmed as partnership schools, and 17 attended three training days. Feedback was overwhelmingly positive with many schools reporting changes in practice as a result. Training was provided to schools and other important stakeholders (e.g. paediatricians) on the statutory guidance for supporting learners with medical needs and related topics. Because of the project's work, there were improved links with key groups such as CAMHS, School Health Nursing, and the county inclusion teams – highlighting the presence of the project team and the support available. A direct pathway into Children's Psychological Medicine (CPM) was developed for learners with medical needs experiencing difficulties within education; this improved accessibility to psychology and integrated psychology in the use of Individual Healthcare Plans. The year 1 pilot also saw developments in the support of clinical psychology to OHS directly, to aid with assessment processes, liaison with appropriate external agencies, and provision of training and consultation, within the remit of the psychologist's role.

It was clear that there was a real lack of understanding and training around even the basics of the statutory guidance from most stakeholders.

The psychological input (see also Chapter 7)

Managing the psychological and emotional health of learners with medical needs in a way that maximises their educational integration can be a complicated task. Identifying barriers to providing excellent care, armed with limited information from the child's clinical care team, it can be difficult to make judgements about aspects of school life. From gathering information from clinical teams to form an effective plan, to considering the impact on teachers of managing complex and sometimes emotive situations, the psychology-focused arm of the project aimed to help educators develop robust pathways for supporting learners with medical needs. Project partners were provided with the theoretical and best practice knowledge that informs practical and creative suggestions for how to best implement the guidance available.

Dr Helen Griffiths led the psychology strand of the project, working to create an evidence-based framework for achieving good educational outcomes for learners with medical needs. She described her work as being focused on improving the experiences of these learners through creating a permanent community of teaching and health professionals.

Dr Konrad Jacobs, a Consultant Paediatric Clinical Psychologist commented:

'The reality is that health and education don't often talk to each other, and that means we miss opportunities to support these learners by collaborating with their teachers'. He went on to say:

> This project is so important because it's all about closing the loop between health and education. It's about putting in place simple ways of working together and giving teachers the confidence to interpret and accommodate a child's physical and mental symptoms. One of the biggest areas of uncertainty among teachers is to what extent the school needs to adapt to accommodate a pupil's medical needs. As a rule, the less you adapt and the more you stick to a routine the better for the child. With training and clear channels to professional advice, teachers can make proactive decisions on issues like this.

Self-reflection

- How strongly do you encourage a learner with medical needs to participate?
- How can you identify when they have had enough?
- How do you manage them feeling different from their peers?
- How could their medical teams support you in making these decisions?

The project began delivering face-to-face training for a small group of schools as part of an initial trial in Oxfordshire and was followed by the first conference in November 2018. Although this was intended to be for Oxfordshire schools, the conference unexpectedly drew a national audience.

By the end of year 1, the project achieved several key impacts assessed by informal verbal feedback, structured evaluation, and outcome measures:

- Overwhelmingly positive feedback from partnership schools on the utility of the training days, leading to a change in practice at many schools. All partnership schools now have a medical needs policy and are using

Individual Healthcare Plans. Some schools have made concrete changes to support learners with medical needs and other vulnerable learners and reported that having access to direct support from the project team was helpful.

- Schools reported that condition-specific information on mental health and psychological formulations of this, teaching on gender identity, individual case studies, discussions with colleagues, communication skills training, and the opportunities to share best practice have been of most help.
- Highlighting areas of need that schools would like additional support with, which will help to shape year 2 priorities and allow feedback to other relevant organisations.
- Increased awareness and use of the statutory and best practice guidance within non-partnership schools who have encountered the MNIS project through other mechanisms (e.g. word-of-mouth, OHS referrals).
- Increased awareness among hospital staff of the challenges facing professionals supporting learners with medical needs in schools, and the input that is needed from health professionals to ensure appropriate plans and supports are in place. This includes the initiation and contribution to IHCPs from health professionals.
- Increased awareness from schools of local services that can support them, including developing links with the CAMHS Inreach Project (supporting learners in their homes).
- Increased and more timely direct support for learners with medical needs with school-related difficulties.
- Direct psychology input into the OHS referrals, assessment, and professional pathway arms of OHS provision.
- Strengthened networks with key stakeholders – school health nursing, CAMHS, inclusion leads, SENCOs, etc.

Year 2 of the project

The pilot project entered its second year in September 2018 and sharpened its focus on the key aims.

It was clear that many learners were not accessing optimal learning alongside their classmates because their schools were not adequately supported to adapt to their medical condition and associated psychological needs. Keeping learners safe and comfortable must be a priority, but too often, OHS staff were seeing that a lack of training and a fear of making the learner's health worse would lead to them being withdrawn from classroom teaching. In some cases, learners who should have had access to full-time education were being home-schooled or were put on part-time or virtual learning timetables because their condition was being misunderstood or poorly managed.

We wanted to give schools the tools and the confidence to help these learners to be fully included and integrated in their school or college communities.

As the new headteacher at Oxfordshire Hospital School when the project embarked on its second year, I became by default part of this exciting and pioneering initiative. I had moved from 28 years of teaching in the main-stream sector with most of my experience in pastoral leadership roles. I had been that mainstream school leader who didn't know what to do, and who wanted a medical professional on call to discuss learners' health concerns; I'd been the person who talked about inclusion, who was evangelical about it in my school but who was, if I'm honest, somewhat lost for ideas when it came to supporting the education of learners with chronic health condi-tions. I wanted to do more, I wanted to do better, but I did not know how or where to start.

With an incredibly dedicated and specialist team around me, I quickly learned that there are steps that every school can take to ensure they are doing their best for learners and meeting their moral and legal obligation to give every learner access to high-quality learning regardless of medical need.

The MNIS team continued to provide face-to-face training, including a second successful conference. The project was going well, and we were not only supporting education professionals locally by building networks and enhancing knowledge, but we were also building a growing appetite for the work of the Medical Needs in Schools (MNIS) project nationally.

The responsibility of other stakeholders

Interestingly, the duty to support learners with medical conditions applies to health as well as education, although schools tend to feel responsibility falls predominantly on their side. There are many healthcare professionals and charities who will offer advice to schools on how to support learners (see Chapter 16); for example, the school nursing team can be an essential resource in the planning stages.

The development of the online learning platform

When the pandemic hit, we knew we had some decisions to make. We could not continue with our schedule of face-to-face training, but we knew people still wanted the training; so, like everyone else during the pandemic, we launched our online offer. Initially, we provided live training events hosted using our network of contacts to invite professionals from Oxfordshire schools. We used previous contact information to ensure that every school in the authority was informed about training events and guidance.

Lockdowns meant that some school staff had more time for training too, but of course, not all at the same time. To make this accessible to all staff, we recorded our training and posted these online. Consequently, we created a bank of training videos that contained some great resources but that were a bit amateurish. We then collaborated with the company Aspire2Be (https://aspire2be.co.uk/home/), who had the skills to develop a specialist site for us to host our training. We launched the MNIS training site (https://medicalneedsinschools.co.uk/) and our partners at Aspire2Be had done us proud. We were amateurs when it came to producing training videos but with their guidance and highly-skilled approach, we were able to polish our clumsy attempts into something professional. We were impressed!

We wanted the idea of the training site and its potential to embed itself in the minds of school leaders, local authority leaders, and professionals representing various health conditions from within the NHS and the charitable sector. We wanted to build a set of useful, usable resources that colleagues would learn from, that would change practice, which would improve educational outcomes for learners with medical conditions.

By this point, the site had become a one-stop shop of 17 courses highlighting best practice for supporting learners with medical conditions including anxiety, asthma, acquired brain injury, bowel and bladder conditions, cancer, heart disease, and self-harm. We liaised and collaborated with other charities and key professionals to access their training materials as there was no need to replicate what had already been put in place. By 2023, the National Acquired Brain Injury In Learning And Education Syndicate, the Child Brain Injury Trust, Oxford Health NHS Trust, Oxfordshire Education Psychology Service, Young Minds, Oxfordshire GPs, Oxford University Hospitals NHS Trust, Little Hearts Matter, and Long Covid Kids had all contributed along with colleagues from the OHS (see also Chapter 16).

By June 2023, only 18 months since its soft launch and only a month following its official launch, the site had received 46,000 visits from 3,600 users in 38 different countries!

The original plans to make the project scalable were well founded. The Northamptonshire Hospital and Outreach Education team joined the MNIS project, launching their site in early 2024, and there are plans to bring on another partner in the Midlands for their official launch in Autumn 2024.

Self-reflection

- Where can you access relevant training and support in your local area?
- Have you checked out the MNIS site?
- Consider how you could make use of the training, resources, and information on the site to support the practice in your school.

Peter Drucker (2006) is famous for saying that 'Culture eats strategy for breakfast'. I am sure some might argue this, but in the context of school inclusion, there is no better statement. There is a way to achieve this and a challenge to maintain it, but it is essential. Only then will you achieve the culture of inclusion that you want. Schools are using these training resources as part of their annual training programmes for staff. They have changed their policies and are far more aware of the need to not just say they are inclusive but to be inclusive. I firmly believe that everyone that works in education wants the best outcomes for learners. These training resources help them to achieve some of the aspirational and inclusive goals that education professionals set for themselves.

5 top tips

1. It starts with **policy** – what are you going to do?
2. Then you need to **train** your staff. They need to know why they are doing it.
3. Next you make them **accountable**. Everyone needs to be on board.
4. What we do, what we say, must be **aspirational** and inclusive for young people with medical conditions.
5. Make it a habit – make it routine.

Index

Page numbers in **bold** refer to tables.

acquired brain injury (ABI): challenges in childhood 94–5; challenges of education provision 95–6; class-based interventions 101–2, **104–6**; cumulative impact of 103; definition of 93; difficulties *94*; neuro-fatigue *94*, 103; returning to education after 97–8, *99*; school as rehabilitation environment 96–7; starting education with 97; targeted approach 102; top tips 107–8; transition between schools 100; whole school approaches 100–2; Young Experts by Experience (YEBEABI) 92–3
acute illness/condition, definition of 130
additional educational needs (AENs) 36–7
ADHD and autism 86–7
adrenaline auto-injectors 123, 124–5
Allergy UK 174–5
anaphylaxis 123, 124–5
Anaphylaxis UK 175–6
anxiety: identifying causes of 82; medical condition and procedures 56–7; missed education 65; reintegration 138–9, 140; social situations 67–8; stigma of psychiatric admission 167; *see also* Child and Adolescent Mental Health Units (CAMHS)
anxiety disorder (case study/Shiva) 141–2
assessments: of need 65–7; staff administration of medicines 116
asthma attacks 123, 124
attachment styles 58
autism and ADHD 86–7
AV1 robot 72–3; benefits of use 73–4, 137; in CAMHS units 165; case studies 76–9; potential challenges 74–6; top tips 79

Bannon, M.J and Ross, E.M 121–2
behaviours: as communication 86–8; neurodiversity and additional educational needs (AENs) 36–7
belonging/connection 74, 98, 156–7, 165, 166
bone cancer (case study/Niall) 142–3
brain plasticity 94
bullying 38, 44, 144

cardiopulmonary resuscitation (CPR) 123

Child and Adolescent Mental Health Units (CAMHS) 161–2; hospital school: communication and collaboration 163–4; learner concerns 165–8; parent/carer concerns 168–9; planning for discharge and reintegration 164; purpose of 162–3; reintegration (case studies) 141–2, 143–4; Tier 4 Schools 36, 64; top tips 170

Children and Families Act (2014) 9, 115

Children's Act (1989) 84

children's health charities 173–83

Children's Heart Federation 176–7

Children's Psychological Medicine (CPM) 186

Clinical Commissioning Groups see Integrated Care Boards

clothing 89–90

collaboration/partnership: CAMHS units 163–4; external professionals/agencies 66, 159; hospital school/medical AP and reintegration 137, 138, 139, 141, 145; identifying learner needs 82–3; paediatric hospitals 153–4; see also medicines management; parents/carers

colorectal surgery (case study/Jasmin) 49

communication: behaviours as 86–8; CAMHS units 163–4; reintegration support 33–5, 140; transitioning home from paediatric hospital 159; see also information access/sharing; learner voices; parents/carers

community pharmacies see pharmacies

competency assessments, staff administration of medicines 116

concentration issues 50, 57

confidentiality and sensitivity 15

connection-seeking behaviour (case studies/Sharon and David) 87–8

connection/belonging 74, 98, 156–7, 165, 166

consent, medicines management 113–14, 120

COVID-19 pandemic 31; Lond Covid Kids (LCK) 177–8; long-term effects (case study/Bailey) 78–9; online learning platform 190–1

creative exploration/approaches 68–9, 89

curriculum: quality of education 35–6; see also wider curriculum

Datapharm, Medicines Compendium (eMC) 127

deficit vs growth mindset language 36–7

Department for Education (DfE) 9; AV1 robots 73; IHCPs 18; medical emergencies 123; medical and mental health conditions 55; SEND and AP Green Paper 81; SEND Code of Practice: 0–25 years 84

Department of Health: adrenaline auto-injectors 124–5; emergency salbutamol inhalers 124

development milestones 57–8

dextrose/glucose tablets 123

diabetes (case study/Mariam) 48–9

dialysis inpatient (case study/Rowan) 157–8

'difference', sense of 57

disruptive/dysregulated learner (case study/Arlo) 87
Drucker, P. 191
dual registration 25–6

eating disorder (case study/Courtney) 143–4
Education Act (1966), LAs and Section 19 responsibilities 24–5
Education Act (1993), medicines management 122
emotional and social support 61; transitioning home from paediatric hospital 159
emotionally based school avoidance (EBSA)/non-attendance (EBSNA) 44, 86
English Baccalaureate (EBacc) 35
enteric feeding tubes 130
epileptic seizures 123
exams: CAMHS unit 166–7; case study (Mariam) 48–9; future/career focus 46; responsibility for arrangements 26
external agencies/professionals 66, 159

fatigue 57; acquired brain injury (ABI) 94, 103
First Aid at Work training 123
Fletcher, M. et al. 73
flexible education pathway 45
functional neurological disorder/ conversion disorder (case study/ Anne) 76–7
future/career focus 46

glucose/dextrose tablets 123
Google Classroom 75

governing bodies, role of 10
gradual exposure and small steps 138–9
Great Ormond Street Hospital 153
Griffiths, H. 184–5, 186–7
growth mindset 36–7

headteachers (roles and responsibilities) 12; administration of medicines 115; IHCP 19
Health Conditions in Schools Alliance 173–4
health services, roles and responsibilities of 13
healthcare professionals (roles and responsibilities) 13; and external professionals/agencies 66, 159; IHCP 19, 22; specialist nurses 139, 159; see also medicines management; school nurse
high-stakes testing 35
Hopwood, V. et al. 42
hospital schools see Child and Adolescent Mental Health Units (CAMHS); medical Alternative Provision (AP)/hospital school; Medical Needs in Schools project; paediatric hospitals; wider curriculum
hypoglycaemia 123

identification: of key adults 141; of learner needs 82–3; of medical condition 13–14
immunosuppression (case study/Joshi) 77–8
individual healthcare plans (IHCPs): administration of medicines 114, 122, 123; contents 20–1; definition

of 17–18; development process 21–2; reintegration support following absence 139–40; responsibilities 18–19; reviews 22; transition between schools 22–3

information access/sharing: acquired brain injury (ABI) 96, 100; AV1 robot 75; from learners *see* learner voices; hospital staff 151; medicines 126–8, 129

infusion pumps 131

Integrated Care Boards (Clinical Commissioning Groups), roles and responsibilities of 13

intrathecal catheter 131

Jacobs, Dr K. 187

Jim, J. et al. 94–5

key adults: identification of 141; *see also* named person

key needs 2–3

leadership: and culture 32; within and outside classroom 154

learner voices: asking the right questions 83–4; best practice in listening to 84–5, 88–9; Child and Adolescent Mental Health Units (CAMHS) 165–8; long-term physical health conditions (LTPHCs) 42–4; reintegration support 137–8

learners (roles and responsibilities) 12; IHCP 19; self-administration 122–3; self-management 14

legal requirements 9–10; actions following identification of medical condition 13–14; governing bodies, role of 10; school policy, developing 10–12; school staff and other stakeholders, roles and responsibilities of 12–13; self-management, role of learner 14; sensitivity and confidentiality 15; *see also* medicines management

leukaemia (case study/Billy) 47–8

life skills and transition 69

listening *see* learner voices

local authority (LA) responsibilities 13; alternative provision (AP), arrangements and referral 25–6; parent/carer collaboration 26; statutory 24–5; supporting learner on return to school 26

local pharmacies *see* pharmacies

Lond Covid Kids (LCK) 177–8

long-term physical health conditions (LTPHCs) 41; case studies 47–9; common needs impacting attendance 44–6; context 41–2; INSCHOOL research study 42; learner views 42–4; practical, cost-effective strategies 50–2; top tips 52–3

LUPUS UK 178–9

marginalisation 43

medical Alternative Provision (AP)/ hospital school 81–2; case studies 87–9; identifying learner needs 82–3; local authority (LA) arrangements and referral 25–6; observed behaviours as communication 86–7; partnership in reintegration 137, 138, 139, 141, 145; practical solutions for other school

pressures 89–90; support and interventions 85–6; top tips 90
medical emergencies 123–4
medical errors 125–6
Medical Needs in Schools project 36, 184–5; aims 185; online learning platform 190–1; stakeholder responsibilities 189–90; top tips 192; Year 1 185–6; Year 2 188–9
medicines: definition of 131; non-prescription/OTC 120, 127; 'off-label'/'unlicensed' 127, 131–2
Medicines Administration Record (MAR) chart 121
Medicines Compendium (eMC), Datapharm 127
medicines management 110; access to information 126–8, 129; administration 14–15, 119–21; best practice requirements 119, 126; consent 113–14, 120; glossary 130–1; importance for schools 110; labelling 117, 118; learner self-administration 122–3; legislation and policy development 14–15, 111–13, 121–2; legislative changes to support schools 124–5; local pharmacies 125, 128–9; medical emergencies 123–4; medical errors 125–6; specific challenges for schools 111; staff training 115–17, 121, 123; storage 117–19; top tips 129–30
medium secure units 163, 166–7
mental health: and medical conditions 55; positive 46; support and resilience 67; see also anxiety; Child and Adolescent Mental Health Units (CAMHS)

midazolam, buccal 123
Mintz, J. et al. 153
mobile/smartphones 37–8, 48–9, 163, 165

named person 11, 151; see also key adults
National ABI in Learning and Education Syndicate (NABLES) 92–3, 98
neuro-fatigue 94, 103
neurodiversity 36–7
neuropsychiatric disorders (PANS PANDAS UK) 179–80

off rolling 167–8
Ofsted: definition of wider curriculum 64; roles and responsibilities of 13
Oxford Hospital School 152; see also Medical Needs in Schools project

Paediatric First Aid training 123
paediatric hospitals 149; case study 157–8; clinical settings 149–50; collaborative learning - expectations and strategies 153–4; delivering education to inpatient 151–2; parent/carer roles and communication 155, 159; relationships within and outside classroom 154; and schools, compared 150; sharing 156–7; top tips 160; transitioning home 158–60; visits 157
pain 57
PANS PANDAS UK 179–80
parents/carers: benefits of AV1 robot 74; concerns regarding CAMHS 168–9; IHCP 19, 22; medicines, management and

administration 113–14, 120, 128–9;
paediatric hospitals, admission
and transitioning home 155, 159;
reintegration support 34–5, 140;
roles and responsibilities 12
partnerships see collaboration/
partnership; medicines management;
parents/carers
patient information leaflets (PILs) 127
peers see connection/belonging
percutaneous endoscopic gastrostomy
(PEG) feeding tube 130
pharmacies 125, 127, 128–9
physical activity and recreation 68
physical health conditions see long-
term physical health conditions
(LTPHCs)
physical impact of medical
condition 57
positive mental health 46
post traumatic stress disorder 34, 37
principles and key needs 1–3
psychiatric treatment see Child and
Adolescent Mental Health Units
(CAMHS)
psychological impact 54; case studies
59–61; cognitive and behavioural
58–9; demands of management
of medical condition 56–7;
development milestones 57–8;
journey to diagnosis 55–6; medical
conditions and mental health
55; physical impact of medical
condition 57; positives 58; practical,
cost-effective strategies 61; self-
esteem and mood 57; top tips 61–2
pupil passports 100

quality of education 35–6

Ransby, A. 184–5
'Recovery Curriculum' 35
reintegration support 135–6;
approaches 136–7; CAMHS 164;
case studies 141–4; communication
33–5, 140; gradual exposure and
small steps 138–9; IHCP 139–40;
key adults, identification of 141;
learner voices 137–8; partnership
working 137; school as best
place for learning 144–5; top
tips 146; see also welcoming
environment
Royal College of Paediatrics and Child
Health (RCPCH) 127
Royal Pharmaceutical Society 121

safe management of health at
school 44
safety plans, CAMHS 164, 166
salbutamol inhalers 123, 124
school nurse (roles and responsibilities)
12–13; IHCP 19, 22, 139
school policy, developing 10–12
school prom 166
school staff see staff
self-esteem: benefits of AV1 robot
73–4; and mood 57
self-harm risk/behaviours: case study
(Evie) 37–8; school prom 166
SENCOs 167
SEND Code of Practice: 0–25 years
(DfE) 84
sensitivity and confidentiality 15
Shier, H. 84–5

situational mutism 68; creative approaches 89
smartphones/mobile phones 37–8, 48–9, 163, 165
social situations: benefits of AV1 robot 73–4; wider curriculum 67–8
specialist nurses 139, 159
staff: benefits and challenges of AV1 robot 73, 74, 75; and other stakeholders, roles and responsibilities of 12–13; visits to paediatric hospitals 157
staff training: brain development and injury 100; medicines management 115–17, 121, 123
stigma 167
syringe driver 131

teachers *see* staff
technology: information gathering from learners 89, 137–8; online learning platform, OHS 190–1; policy development templates 112–13, 174; websites for information on medicines 126–8; *see also* AV1 robot; smartphones/mobile phones
Tier 4 CAMHS Schools 36, 64
timetables, reduced 90, 138

transition: between schools 22–3, 100; hospital to home 158–60; life skills and 69

Versus Arthritis 180–1

welcoming environment 31–2; behaviour, neurodiversity, and additional educational needs (AENs) 36–7; case study (Evie) 37–8; communication and relationships 33–5; leadership and culture 32; quality of education 35–6; top tips 38
Well at School 182–3
'What Matters Island' template 89
wider curriculum 63; assessment of need 65–7; context of Becton School 63–4; creative exploration 68–9; impact of 69–70; life skills and transition 69; mental health support and resilience 67; physical activity and recreation 68; social situations 67–8; top tips 70–1

Young Epilepsy 181–2
Young Experts by Experience (YEBEABI) 92–3